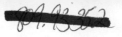

809.93352
Sta

Standen, Rodney

The changing face of the
hero $6.95

THE CHANGING FACE OF THE HERO

RODNEY STANDEN

A Quest Book

*This publication made possible with
the assistance of the Kern Foundation*

The Theosophical Publishing House
Wheaton, Ill. U.S.A.
Madras, India / London, England

A Quest original. First edition, 1987

The Theosophical Publishing House
306 West Geneva Road
Wheaton, IL 60187

A publication of the Theosophical Publishing House, a department of the Theosophical Society in America.

Library of Congress Cataloging in Publication Data

Standen, Rodney, 1937-
   The changing face of the hero.

   (A Quest Book)
   Based on the author's thesis (Ph.D.)
   Bibliography: p.
   Includes index.
   1. Heroes in literature. 2. Self-realization in literature.
3. Archetype (Psychology) I. Title.
PN56.5.H45S7 1987   809′.93352   86-40404
ISBN 0-8356-0616-3 (pbk.)

Printed in the United States of America

To Ilene, my wife and best friend,
who made it happen

Contents

Acknowledgments

The author wishes to thank the following publishers for permission to quote material from their publications:

Approximately 25 lines passim from "Howl" in *Collected Poems 1947-1980* by Allen Ginsberg. Copyright (c) 1955 by Allen Ginsberg. Reprinted by permission of Harper and Row, Publishers, Inc.

Excerpts reprinted with permission of Princeton University Press, from *The Collected Works of C. G. Jung,* trans. R. F. C. Hull, Bollingen Series XX. Vol. 15: *The Spirit in Man, Art, and Literature.* Copyright (c) 1966 by Princeton University Press.

Excerpts from *The Odyssey: A Modern Sequel,* Nikos Kazantzakis, translated by Kimon Friar. Copyright (c) 1958 by Simon & Schuster, Inc.

Excerpts from *Shadow and Evil in Fairy Tales,* Marie-Louise Von Franz, Spring Publications, 1974.

Introduction

We carry with us the wonders we seek without us.

Sir Thomas Browne

We all travel, if not in space in time. And since the first strolling teller-of-tales enthralled his audience at the first campfire, we have all loved travelers and travelers' tales. From Gilgamesh through Odysseus to Bilbo Baggins and Frodo, the epic journey and its hero continue to capture our imagination. By comparison our own journeys, our own lives, seem uneventful indeed. Then too, most of us only journey without—in outer time and outer space; our inner journeys are confined to those rendered essential, even inevitable, by the very fact of being alive.

Today virtually everyone is aware of psychology and psychiatry—aware, therefore, of at least the possibility of an inner journey; aware, even if the names are not immediately familiar, of individuation and Self-realization. We are increasingly excited and fascinated by the inner journey—and perhaps a little afraid of all that is implied.

Our new fascination is perhaps nowhere better illustrated than in the changing face of the modern hero of the western world. Yesterday's John Wayne could punch and sashay his way across the western plains; today's John Wayne is a master of martial arts, a virtually indestructible Ninja. No Superman, but almost "able to leap tall buildings with a single bound." And as a Ninja, or master of Kung Fu, we know that our hero has had not only to steel his body but to steel his mind as well. He can recite koans. He is wise. He can see not only the beauty, but the strength in a single rose petal. He has sat at the feet of a master. He has journeyed within.

Once again the old saw is proven true: change comes not from above, but from below. The empty but lethal hand of Kung Fu has prepared the ground for the esoteric koan of Zen Buddhism. In the pages of comic books, paperbacks, and on movie screens, East and West have moved closer together. This is nowhere better illustrated than in the most popular hero of a generation, arguably the most popular of all time: Luke Skywalker.

In most cases we have no way of knowing the genesis of popular heroes; but we do exactly know the genesis of Luke Skywalker, indeed of the "Star Wars" cycle. George Lucas has acknowledged his debt to Joseph Campbell, going so far as to arrange a special screening of his trilogy in order that Campbell might see how closely it followed the path of *The Hero With A Thousand Faces*.

> "The Call to Adventure," or the signs of the vocation of the hero; "Refusal of the Call," or the folly of the flight from the god; "Super-

natural Aid," the unsuspected assistance that comes to one who has undertaken his proper adventure; "The Crossing of the First Threshold"; "The Belly of the Whale," or the passage into the realm of night..."The Road of Trials," or the dangerous aspect of the gods... "Atonement with the Father"; "Apotheosis"; and "The Ultimate Boon"..."The Crossing of the Return Threshold," or the return to the world of common day; "Master of the Two Worlds"; "Freedom to Live," the nature and function of the ultimate boon. (5, p. 36)

Such is the path of Campbell's hero; such, too, is the path of Luke Skywalker.

But Campbell has also written:

Whether we listen with aloof amusement to the dreamlike mumbo jumbo of some red-eyed witch doctor of the Congo, or read with cultivated rapture thin translations from the sonnets of the mystic Lao-tse; now and again crack the hard nutshell of an argument of Aquinas, or catch suddenly the shining meaning of a bizarre Eskimo fairy tale, it will be always the one, shape-shifting yet marvelously constant story that we find. (5, p. 3)

At first glance, therefore, the contention that the face of the western hero has changed, and is changing still, would seem to contradict Campbell and his monomyth.[1] In fact the converse is true: if the face of the western hero is changing, is assum-

---

[1] Joseph Campbell uses "Monomyth" extensively in connection with his thousand-faced hero; however, in a footnote on p. 30 he points out that the word was originally used by James Joyce in *Finnegan's Wake*.

ing a more eastern cast, then Campbell's thesis is reinforced, rather than contradicted.

Given its genesis it should come as no surprise that the "Star Wars" trilogy abounds in Jungian archetypes.[2] Before Luke has to confront his actual shadow it is possible to accept Han Solo as his shadow-figure and Chewbaccaa as Han's shadow. Princess Leia is a classic anima figure. Jung would, I'm certain, applaud Luke's first glimpse of her; for as projected by R2D2 she is a shimmering, dreamlike figure. And then there is Obi-Wan Kenobi, if not divine, at least semi-divine, if not a Self figure, at least a very wise old man; and his wisdom comes, not from an anthropomorphised western god, but from "The Force." "The Force"—Paramatma.[3] East and West have come together; and for Obi-wan Kenobi it is not death that awaits, but apotheosis.

But what of our hero? What of Luke Skywalker? In the course of his inner and outer journeyings he

---

[2]Both Self-realization and individuation play important roles in *The Changing Face of The Hero*. The former is virtually self-explanatory. Self-realization is literally that: man's realization of his Self—his higher Self—i.e., becoming all that he can be and living life on a day-to-day basis as all that he can be, thereby realizing, from moment to moment, the fullness of his potential. The Jungian concept of individuation is not dissimilar. On the journey to the Jungian Self one encounters such figures as the shadow and the anima; and we will encounter these figures as we examine the changing face of the Hero. The reader unfamiliar with these terms will find them well defined in *Man And His Symbols*, a book edited by C.G. Jung and published by Doubleday.

[3]*Paramatma*. Sometimes, *Paramatman* (Sanskrit). The Supreme Soul of the universe. From *Para/Param* and *Atma/Atman*. Para

has acquired a light-sword and an indomitable will power; furthermore, he has confronted and come to terms with Jung's archetypes. But he has also contacted, not merely his Atma, but Paramatma—"The Force." He too, then, is an amalgam of East and West.

To understand the hero, his changing, and some-times unchanging face, we must leave Luke Sky-walker and travel back twenty-five hundred and more years to Ancient Greece. There we find the most famous hero of them all—a long distance traveler who has almost certainly captured the im-agination of more readers, in more countries, in more times, than any other character in world literature.

Like all those playing starring roles in this study, this character is masculine. Our study is called *The Changing Face of the Hero*, not *The Changing Face of the Heroine*. To the uninitiated this might suggest that the face of the heroine has not changed, or else that female persons do not individuate and could not possibly experience Self-realization. Obviously this is not true. What is true, however, is that, with some notable exceptions (very few) lit-erature has always been more concerned with male characters than with females. For century upon century it has been culturally acceptable for the male hero to be errant, in every meaning of the

---

is the "Infinite" and "Supreme" in philosophy—the final limit. Param is the end and goal of existence. *Atma* (or *Atman*) is the Universal Spirit, the divine Monad, the 7th Principle in the septenary constitution of man. The Supreme Soul. Vide H.P. Blavatsky. *Theosophical Glossary* (3).

word, while the female heroine waits. She either waits at home for the return of her hero, or in some dragon's lair for rescue by her hero.

Our culture accepts, in fact expects, that the hero, more or less active, be masculine, and the heroine, more or less passive, be feminine. But our culture accepts more than this. It accepts that consciousness and spirit are masculine, earth and matter feminine. In this sense, the face of the hero is a metaphor for the spirit of humankind; and humankind is comprised of women as well as men.

In his book *The Great Mother* Erich Neumann, Jungian analyst and author of *The Psychic Development of the Feminine,* talks about the relation of the son to the Great Mother, of the symbolic struggle between the mother and the male child, and of how the increasing strength of the child corresponds to the increasing power of human consciousness. He then makes it clear that, although the struggle in question is between mother and son, it could as well take place between mother and daughter. The symbolic struggle is between matter and consciousness, and consciousness is masculine, whether housed in son or daughter.

In short, individuation and Self-realization are for everybody; and the face of the hero is the face of all who tread the path of expanding consciousness—of all sons and daughters of Grandfather Sky and Grandmother Earth.

1

The Archetype of a Hero
(Homer, *The Odyssey*, I)

*Odysseus' long voyage home has become a paradigm
for the journey of self-discovery which finally leads
back, after many trials and confrontations with
strange humans, monsters, gods, and giants, to the
center where one really belongs.*
                    Sallie Nichols, Jung and Tarot

Odysseus' name gave the language a new word,
and that word has come to mean much more than
merely a long journey—even a journey back to the
"center where one really belongs." Odyssey. It is
hard to think of a better example of one of Noam
Chomsky's "hairy words."[1] It comes supercharged
with concepts and implications. But surely the
main concept, and the one most likely to spring to
the mind of a modern reader, is that of the inner
journey. "It was a personal odyssey." "This trip
really changed my life. It was, you know, like an
odyssey." When twentieth century man speaks of
an odyssey, he is referring, not to a great trek, but
to a voyage of self-discovery—a journey *within*.

---

[1]To Noam Chomsky, founding father of Transformational
Grammar, a "hairy" word is one rich with implications and
connotations—an evocative word. To most of us, "tandem"
would probably be hairier than "bicycle"; both "cottage" and
"villa" almost certainly say more than "house"; and to prac-
tically everyone the hyphenate "Rolls-Royce" would conjure
images far beyond any which could be evoked by the simple
monosyllable "car."

Indeed it could be argued that this latter has become the accepted modern meaning of the word, that the meaning has changed, and that change has, for the most part, occurred in the twentieth century. The *Oxford English Dictionary* defines the "Odyssey" as, "a long series of wanderings to and fro, a long adventurous journey." It reinforces the definition with examples of usage that end in 1899. These include such passages as, "The odysseys of historical (music) scores might form the subject of an interesting volume." *Webster's Third International Dictionary* defines "odyssey" as "an intensive intellectual or spiritual wandering or quest," and gives as examples of usage, "the emotional odyssey of an intelligent and romantic young girl," and "less a historical novel than the story of a spiritual odyssey." The Oxford dictionary provides a definition in keeping with the last century's usage, whereas Webster's confirms the shift in the meaning of the word from an outward adventure to an inward quest.

At irregular intervals in this book, I will refer to time in terms of ripeness, i.e., of events which happen when the world is ready for them to happen, or perhaps, when the world needs them to happen. The change in meaning of the word "odyssey" is a good example of this ripeness. At some time between the 1890s and the 1960s the world, or enough of the world to matter, became aware that man's journey was not merely through new lands and new times, but through himself, and that this inner journey was potentially the greatest odyssey of all.

"But though masquerading as an epic, the
Odyssey is the first Greek novel; and therefore
wholly irresponsible where myths are concerned."
(11, p. 376) Robert Graves may well be unique in
accusing the Odyssey of masquerading as an epic,
but he is certainly not the first to suggest that this
is the first Greek novel—indeed the first novel. For
our purpose this is all to the good. It is hard to
equate gods, or even demigods, with such human
voyages as those of individuation or Self-realization; their proportions are too Olympian by far.
Nor should we overconcern ourselves with the
work's genesis, the probable remolding of two
legends to fit one hero, and the intriguing possibility that *The Odyssey* was authored, not by Homer,
but by a Sicilian noblewoman, who, it has been
suggested, modelled the character of Nausicaa on
herself.

Our story, however, begins before the first page
of *The Odyssey*, even before the opening lines of
Homer's earlier epic poem, *The Iliad*.

> This Odysseus, though he passed as the son of
> Laertes, had been secretly begotten by
> Sisyphus on Anticleia, daughter of the famous
> thief, Autolycus (11, p. 278).

In fact Sisyphus and Autolycus were neighbors; in
typical neighborly fashion, the latter was rustling
the cattle of the former. However, while visiting
his good neighbor in order to confront him with
proof of his crime, Sisyphus was distracted by the
beauty of Anticleia.

9

Given a famous thief for a maternal grandfather
and a father whose connivings were such that, for
a while, he even managed to cheat Death himself,
it is perhaps not surprising that Odysseus was, to
say the least, a great strategist; indeed were we to
employ dysphemism rather than euphemism we
might simply call our hero a con man. But perhaps
we should applaud rather than judge. The cliché
tells us that the Devil gets all the best songs, and
the song of Odysseus is very good indeed.

Our hero had been warned by an oracle that
should he journey to Troy he would not return for
twenty years, and even then he would be alone
and destitute. In the circumstances, his reluctance
to volunteer is understandable; and this reluctance
introduces us to the strategist, the master of disguise, the trickster.

When Agamemnon, Menalaus, and Palamedes
arrive at Ithaca in order to draft Odysseus, he
feigns madness. He pretends not to recognize his
guests, dons a peasant's cap shaped like a half
egg, and with an ox and an ass yoked together,
ploughs a field, and sows it with salt. Palamedes,
however, places Telemachus, Odysseus' infant
son, directly in the path of the oncoming plough.
In order to avoid killing his only son, Odysseus
hastily reins in. His sanity thus proven, he has no
alternative but to join the expedition.

Some authorities have suggested that we do
Odysseus an injustice if we believe that his

charade was intended merely to save himself from
bearing arms in the Trojan War:

> Odysseus' pretended madness, though con-
> sistent with his novel reluctance to act as
> behoved a king, seems to be misreported.
> What he did was to demonstrate prophetically
> the uselessness of the war to which he had
> been summoned. Wearing a conical hat which
> marked the mystagogue or seer, he ploughed a
> field up and down. Ox and ass stood for Zeus
> and Cronus, or summer and winter; and each
> furrow, sown with salt, for a wasted year.
> Palamedes, who also had prophetic powers,
> then seized Telemachus and halted the plough,
> doubtless at the tenth furrow, by sitting him in
> front of the team: he thereby showed that the
> decisive battle, which is the meaning of 'Tele-
> machus,' would take place then. (11, p. 287)

To accept this as plausible theory rather than
pleasant fancy is to change the face of our hero,
and to do so even before he has taken the first
step on his voyage of individuation—or non-individuation. Odysseus is, first and foremost, a man
of action. To serve his ends, legitimate or otherwise, he will lie and cheat and adopt the most
elaborate of disguises. Such actions are docu-
mented again and again. At no time, however,
could his actions be described as esoteric: the stag-
ing of elaborate symbols is, quite simply, out of
character. Furthermore, for our hero's "symboliz-
ing" to work, we have to assume the informed co-
operation of Palamedes, who just happens to place
Telemachus in the right spot at the right time. Let

11

us examine this assumption in the light of Odysseus' behavior towards Palamedes nine years later, in the closing years of the Trojan War. To get revenge for Palamedes showing him up for an empty-handed foraging expedition, he makes Palamedes appear a traitor through a plot in which he buries gold under the former's tent and fakes a letter saying that it is bribe money. Palamedes is branded a traitor and stoned to death.

It could be argued that Odysseus' revenge was excessive. But what if our hero was avenging, not only a recent loss of face, but also an old wound— a wound which had been nagging at him for nine long years? After all, were it not for Palamedes having placed Telemachus directly in the path of his plough, his charade might well have proven successful and he would not have gone to war. In a sense Palamedes was, even then, showing Odysseus up; the foraging expedition of nine years later might simply have been the last straw.

This theory seems at least as tenable as that of Odysseus as mystagogue. But whichever may be true, we have now met our hero. A conniving master of disguise he may be, yet his name has become synonymous with the voyage of self-discovery—the journey within. Let us, therefore, briefly look at some incidents in his long journey back to home and hearth. At the end of this outer journey we shall be able to assess the inner journey, that of individuation or Self-realization—if, indeed, such a journey has taken place.

12

2

A Changing Face?
(Homer, *The Odyssey*, II)

Men of Troy, what madness has come over you?
Can you believe the enemy truly gone?
A gift from the Danaans, and no ruse?
Is that Ulysses' way, as you have known him?

> . . .

Have no faith in the horse!
Whatever it is, even when Greeks bring gifts
I fear them, gifts and all.
Virgil, The Aeneid

The defenders of Troy had no illusions about
Ulysses, the Latin name for Odysseus. Laocoon,
the Trojan priest of Apollo, might distrust all gift-
bearing Greeks on general principle, but he is
quite specific about our hero: "Is that *Ulysses'*
way?"

It is the tenth year of the war. Now will all
oracles be proven true. Troy will fall; and thereafter will begin that long, long journey, to which
later generations will give the name of our hero.

It has been suggested that Odysseus is, first and
foremost, a victim of fate, a man "chosen" to
achieve certain goals: a man ready to individuate.
Since we are concerned with Eastern as well as
Western concepts, should we not ask if perhaps
this lifetime, this incarnation, is not the result of

many previous incarnations, and that whatever happens to our hero happens as a result of those incarnations—perhaps in spite of the wishes of his conscious ego?

Joseph Campbell has likened the unwilling hero to the victim of a flood: when the hero's time comes and the call is sounded he may refuse to hear. Should he do so, the events necessary for his development will come to him. If the hero won't go to the flood, then the flood will come to the hero (5, passim).

There is much to suggest that, in the case of Odysseus, this is true. After all, we are dealing with an age when the gods are alive and well and forever interfering in the affairs of men. When Athene complains to her father, Zeus, of Odysseus' many hardships, he replies: "My child, what odd complaints you let escape you. Have you not, you yourself, arranged this matter?" The "Summoner of Cloud" then does some arranging of his own:

> Hermes, you have much practice on our
>   missions,
> go make it known to the softly-braided nymph
> that we, whose will is not subject to error,
> order Odysseus home; let him depart.
> But let him have no company, gods or men,
> only a raft that he must lash together,
> and after twenty days, worn out at sea,
> he shall make land upon the garden isle,
> Skheria, of our kinsmen, the Phaiakians.
> Let these men take him to their hearts in
>   honor

> and berth him in a ship, and send him home,
> with gifts of garments, gold, and bronze—
> so much he had not counted on from Troy
> could he have carried home his share of
>   plunder.
> His destiny is to see his friends again
> under his own roof, in his father's country
>   (16, p. 84)

With such evidence of the Olympians as puppet-masters, it is hard to dispute the argument of Odysseus as victim of fate—of a man given only those experiences deemed necessary to bring his life to its preordained conclusion. With this in mind, and forgetting neither individuation nor Self-realization, let us look at some highlights of our hero's ten years of wandering.

It is not necessary to recount the whole long saga; we are concerned only with such episodes of that journey as affect the individuating, or non-individuating face of our hero. This theme is elucidated by two incidents: an encounter with a giant named Polyphemos and our hero's eventual homecoming.

After some years of adventurous wandering in which there is heavy pillaging as well as interference by the gods, Odysseus and his men lay anchor at the fertile islands of the Cyclops. Armed with a potent wine, Odysseus leads twelve of his men in search of provender. They discover a large cave which is amply stocked with cheese and contains well ordered pens for sheep. Odysseus' men favor stealing as much cheese as they can carry and hastening back to their ships; but their leader, curious as to the identity of this mysterious shepherd, elects to await his return.

The shepherd turns out to be a one-eyed giant named Polyphemos. Such is his imposing size and strength that all thirteen of the intruders in his cave would be incapable of removing the boulder with which he casually blocks the door after having driven his sheep into the cave.

Sensing danger, Odysseus introduces himself as "Nobody," and reminds his host of the laws of hospitality ordained by Zeus for the treatment of travelers. Polyphemos, however, has other ideas. Odysseus tells us that

> ...he clutched at my companions
> and caught two in his hands like squirming
>   puppies
> to beat their brains out, spattering the floor.
>
> Then he dismembered them and made his
>   meal,
> gaping and crunching like a mountain lion
> (16, p. 147).

The following morning, after breakfasting on two more men, Polyphemos drives his sheep from the cave and seals the door behind him. In his absence, Odysseus and his men sharpen a large stake and harden its point in the fire. That night, after the giant has dined on two more of his men, Odysseus offers him the strong wine he has with him. So much does the Cyclops enjoy the wine that he tells "Nobody" that, as a reward, he will be the last man to be eaten. In time he falls into a drunken stupor, and Odysseus and his men drive the stake into his single eye.

The blinded giant's screams of agony disturb his neighbors. They gather outside the cave and demand to know what is happening; but when they hear that "Nobody" is tormenting their neighbor, they reason that it must then be the gods, against whom even giants are powerless. They therefore leave Polyphemos to his solitary suffering.

The following morning, when Polyphemos lets his sheep out to graze, the men make their escape by clinging to the thick wool on the undersides of the animals.

Once safely aboard his ship Odysseus yells to Polyphemos:

> if ever mortal man inquire
> how you were put to shame and blinded, tell
>   him
> Odysseus, raider of cities, took your eye:
> Laertes' son, whose home's on Ithaka!
>   (16, p. 154)

In reply Polyphemos raises his hands and prays to his father, Poseidon, god of seas:

> O hear me, lord, blue girdler of the islands,
> if I am thine indeed, and thou art father;
> grant that Odysseus, raider of cities, never
> see his home: Laertes' son, I mean,
> who kept his hall on Ithaka. Should destiny

17

> intend that he shall see his roof again
> among his family in his fatherland,
> far be that day, and dark the years between.
> Let him lose all companions and return
> under strange sail to bitter days at home.
>   (16, p. 155)

As we have already seen, this prayer will be granted.

Were it not for the absence of goddesses, nymphs, or merely mortal concupiscence, we could observe, in this single episode with Polyphemos, every aspect of Odysseus' character. He is courageous; he is resourceful; he is cunning; he is also a braggart and a fool. Telling Polyphemos that his name was "Nobody" was brilliant, but our hero was not content to be brilliant merely in his own eyes and those of his men. Only a braggart or a fool—or both—taunts the son of a god.

This time Odysseus did it to himself. No playful gods pulled the strings. If our hero acted like a puppet, he played the part of the puppet-master too. Or should we consider the Jungian self as puppet-master—pulling the strings which connect it to the conscious ego to prevent that ego from wandering too far from the path of individuation?

Looked at from an oriental standpoint, one could say that one of Odysseus' karmic lessons concerned the overcoming of an over-prickly pride. We are reminded of the hapless Palamedes; and of

18

Eurylokhos, who almost enjoyed a similar fate on Circe's isle:

> Eurylokhos it was, who blurted out:
> Remember those the Kyklops held, remember
> shipmates who made that visit with Odysseus!
> The daring man! They died for his foolishness!

Odysseus responds:

> When I heard this I had a mind to draw
> the blade that swung against my side and chop
>   him,
> bowling his head upon the ground (16, p. 170).

Again it might be suggested that his reaction is a bit excessive.

Later our hero goes on to spend a year in the land (and often in the bed) of the enchantress Circe. Then, after safely navigating past the seductive and dangerous songs of the Sirens, he is shipwrecked by a thunderbolt cast by Zeus himself. The ship is destroyed, and as prophesied, only Odysseus survives. He clings to a spar and is washed ashore on the isle of the nymph Calypso. Many years later, fate, once again in the form of the will of Zeus, will carry him to the court of the king, who will load him down with expensive gifts and see him safely on the last leg of his long homeward journey. He shows his true colors at his homecoming.

Athene, ever Odysseus' greatest champion amongst the immortals, is the first to greet him on his home soil. Having warned him not to go directly to his palace, she disguises him as a beggar and directs him to the hut of the swineherd, Eumaios, who has remained loyal to his missing monarch. She then hastens to the court of Menelaos where she warns Telemachus, who has gone there in search of news of his father, that the evil suitors who have been courting Odysseus' wife Penelope plan to ambush and murder him on his way home.

By following the goddess's instructions, Telemachus comes safely to the hut of Eumaios. At the appropriate moment Athene removes Odysseus' disguise. After embracing, father and son make their plans.

Still disguised as a beggar, Odysseus enters his own palace. There are now over one hundred suitors there. He is recognized by none save an old, old dog and the woman who nursed him as a child. Shortly after his arrival the suitors again insist that Penelope choose from among them.

She agrees to marry the man who can string and draw Odysseus' great bow. She is confident that none will succeed, and is not even present when, with the connivance of Telemachus, the "beggar" is allowed to try—purely for the delectation of the suitors, for who could imagine that this raggedy old tatterdemalion could succeed where so many of the young and strong have already failed?

Jaws drop when the beggar not only strings the bow with ease, but fulfills the rest of Penelope's

test by shooting an arrow through the gap made
by the handles of twelve axes standing in a row.

With Telemachus and Athene at his side,
Odysseus soon destroys all the suitors, disregard-
ing the pleas they offer as soon as they recognize
him. His old nurse tells him that all but twelve of
the palace's fifty maid servants have been faithful—but those twelve have dallied with the suitors.
Odysseus orders these twelve to wash all signs of
carnage from the palace—then he hangs them by
their necks and they, we are told, perished most
piteously.

The hero we have come to know, and yes, to
love, behaves as we have come to expect: he
devises a brilliant stratagem; he assumes a suitable
disguise; he is at once devious and courageous.
(I have always thought that Ovid was being less
than fair when he suggested that Ulysses/Odysseus
was "brave whenever he crossed swords with
timid men" (28, p. 404). In fact he frequently
crossed swords with most un-timid men, and was
just as brave then.)

Seven of Odysseus' ten years of wandering are
spent with the nymph, Calypso, whose bed,
Homer tells us, he shared each and every night.
A year was spent with Circe. In the light of this
behavior, Odysseus' treatment of the twelve maid-
servants unfortunate enough to have sported in
similar fashion with Penelope's suitors might, yet
again, seem excessive. But, as Graves has reminded us, in this un-gentle age women were

seldom regarded as more than possessions, and not very important possessions at that.[1]

Twenty years have passed. Odysseus is home. He has come full circle, or rather, full spiral; for, as countless observers of individuation and Self-realization have pointed out, when it comes to inner growth man proceeds neither in straight lines nor in circles: he follows a spiral path. Hopefully, he spirals upwards. But whether by spiral or by circle, our hero has returned to that point which represents both the start and finish of his odyssey. Has he individuated? Is the vengeful husband who disguises himself as a beggar in order to penetrate the walls of his own home substantially different from the soldier who, ten and more years earlier, disguised himself as a runaway slave in order to penetrate the walls of Troy? Was the young man who feigned madness by sowing salt in his ploughed field less individuated than the older man who hanged twelve maid-servants as punishment for their promiscuity?

No. Like Gertrude Stein's rose, it seems that Odysseus is Odysseus is Odysseus. If our hero has traveled a spiral road, then the loops of that spiral are very, very close together.

Nevertheless, the meaning of the word his name has given to our language will evolve. As we have

---

[1]"The coldblooded treatment of women, suppliants, and allies serves as a reminder that *The Iliad* is not Bronze Age myth... The forced concubinage of Briseis and Chryseis are typical of barbarous saga." Robert Graves, (11, p. 303)

seen, it will increasingly be used to describe the inner, rather than the outer journey of man.

Odysseus too will change. But for him there will be no gradual evolution. He will change suddenly, dramatically, reincarnating first in James Joyce's *Ulysses*, then in Nikos Kazantzakis' continuation of *The Odyssey*.

Myth. Novel. Epic. Call it what you will, *The Odyssey*, whether authored by Samuel Butler's Sicilian noblewoman or Homer, may not tell us much about individuation—except to describe what it is not. But by learning what it is not, may we not learn more of what it is? Furthermore, Odysseus is our most enduring hero. We should study his face, for the same face will be worn by generations of heroes yet unborn. Perhaps by studying it, we will come to better understand *The Odyssey* and appreciate it for what it is. Perhaps too we will sharpen our perspective of individuation and its place in literature. And perhaps, just perhaps, we will come to better understand the spiral of our own lives.

3

The New Heroes

"My name is Bond—James Bond."
Ian Fleming

I have taken as my theme "The Changing Face of The Hero." Having done so, I have quoted extensively from Joseph Campbell's *The Hero With A Thousand Faces*, whose theme is the *un*changing face of the hero. Not content with this, I have recounted some of Homer's *Odyssey*, and concluded that the face of its hero remains pretty much unchanged. I have even suggested that the face of that hero, still unchanged, has been worn, and is still being worn, by whole generations of heroes. Some explanation for this series of seeming contradictions would seem to be called for.

If the face of the Western hero—or of some Western heroes—is changing, then, in order for us to understand that change, we must first understand what it is changing from. Furthermore, it was pointed out in the introduction that *The Odyssey* is not myth but a novel. While much of what Campbell has to say vis-a-vis his thousand-faced hero can be applied to all heroes, he is, nevertheless, basically concerned with heroes of mythic proportions. His work concerns a monomyth, not a mononovel:

> The standard path of the mythological adventure of the hero is a magnification of the formula represented in the rites of passage: *separation—initiation—return:* which might be named the nuclear unit of the monomyth (5, p. 30).

The above lines can easily be applied to Campbell's hero, to the thousand and thousand-thousand heroes whose faces are at once very different and very much the same. Indeed they can be applied not only to heroes, but to most humans, most of whom have been or will be separated, if not from country, from home; if not from family, from the certainties of the very young. This separation marks the entrance to those rites of passage through which we must pass if we are to achieve wholeness—or even partial wholeness.

Sadly, there are some who never survive this journey or emerge from this metaphorical passage. But most do. Ideally we return to fuller life. If so, we have experienced, with at least relative success, some form of initiation, however small that initiation may be. But there are others who return with nothing more than what they left with—and as nothing more than who they were. If they passed through a rite of passage, they were not touched by it; perhaps they have not allowed themselves to be touched by it.

Such is the case with Odysseus. Campbell's lines cannot be applied to him. One third of the formula is missing: he has been separated from Ithaca—he has returned to Ithaca; in the time between, however, no initiation has taken place.

Having followed our own rule and established what Odysseus, and by extension *The Odyssey*, is not, let us try to see it for what it is—a rattling good adventure story full of beautiful women and ugly villains, full, in fact, of sex and violence. Twenty-five hundred years later Odysseus' spiritual great-to-the-nth-degree grandson will introduce himself as "Bond—James Bond."

For who were the fans of this great tale which has lasted for generation upon generation? Students of esoterica in some inner adytum? Or just plain folks who, if alive today, would be following the adventures of James Bond, Travis McGee, J.R. Ewing, and all the heroes of Harold Robbins and his myriad clones?

The Devil gets all the best songs—sometimes! Not when hero and antihero become one. All of the above gentlemen are capable of singing their own ribald ballads. Perhaps this is the secret of their enduring popularity. They might be tougher than we, and braver than we, but, like us, they lie a little, cheat a little, lust a little—or a lot. (James Bond would never waste twelve comely serving wenches, but times and morals have changed— a little.)

26

This then is the "Hero with the Virtually Un-changing Face." He has been with us for thousands of years; doubtless he will remain with us for as long. But center stage may no longer be his exclusive domain; for we have become aware of individuation and Self-realization, and the face of the hero, of some heroes at any rate, is changing.

It could be argued that the face of the hero has always changed, that only the labels have been altered, that individuation and Self-realization have been with us for longer than Odysseus, that, for example, *The Labours of Hercules* can be understood at esoteric levels—even as chapters of a journey within. This is true; but the key word is "esoteric." We would have to search deep in the mists of time to find an age without symbols—an age, therefore, with nothing of the esoteric. But was this level of understanding meaningful to the mass audience, or was Hercules simply a big brave man doing big brave things? We can never know, but I suspect the latter to be the more likely hypothesis.

For better or worse, ours is a media-saturated age; an age, therefore, in which everyone who owns a radio or a T.V. is at least aware of psychology. Today it is possible to be completely illiterate and still have some concept, however hazy, of the "journey within." And one has only to glance at the mushroom growth of psychology to realize how fascinating that journey is to many people. But perhaps it is more than fascinating; perhaps it is important, so important that a new word was needed, a "hairy" word to describe that journey and all that it implied. "Odyssey" suggested itself. It had been around for a few centuries, acquired some vaguely pertinent connotations. With a minimum of restyling it did very nicely.

To understand the changing face of the hero, it is important to understand the changing awareness, the changing needs, of the hero's audience. One has only to live in or visit a fair-sized city to realize immediately how great an impact Eastern concepts have had, and are having, on all our lives—particularly the lives of young people. And one has only to watch, say, forty-eight hours of television to appreciate how interested the viewing public is in inner change. It is epidemic. And it is not the heroes who change; very often they are already at least semiperfect, with perhaps just the odd wart to make them "believable." But keep your eyes on the principal guest stars. Within forty-nine minutes of story and eleven minutes of commercials they will experience instant metanoia: "I'm a better person for having known you, Doctor, Nurse, Policeman, or plain Mister whatever-your-name-is." The point is that if all these T.V. people are changing, they are doing so because that's what the viewers want, or perhaps need—the soap-opera assurance that, not only is change possible, but that guru figures do exist. If not Doctor Kildare, then the Maharishi.

These then are the faces of the hero—the flawed but relatively constant face with which we can all identify, albeit at a relatively less "heroic" level; the face we understand and which, for thousands

of years, has been hugely entertaining. And the
changing face; the individuating, Self-realizing
face, where, perhaps, East and West come together; this face too is often hugely entertaining.
But how many of us can identify with it—how
many would like to? How many of us would like
merely to understand it better, and through it,
perhaps, come better to understand the changing
values of our changing world?

Before time-tripping to walk the streets of Dublin
with an Odysseus reincarnated as Leopold Bloom
in James Joyce's *Ulysses*, we should perhaps examine his non-individuation in more detail.

We have a tendency to automatically confer
something akin to mana on anyone whom we are
told is "well-traveled." We frequently do this
without having met the person in question, and
for no better reason than that he or she may have
some passing familiarity with a sea or cape which
we may never see.

In discussing the axiom of Maria the Prophetess,[1]
Jung has pointed out that in order for the three

---

[1]The axiom of Maria: "One becomes Two, Two becomes
Three, and out of the Third comes One as the Fourth." *The
Collected Works of C.G. Jung.* Volume 13, p. 151. Footnote.

"If we look at this quaternio from the standpoint of the
three-dimensionality of space, then time can be conceived as a
fourth dimension. But if we look at it in terms of the three
qualities of time—past, present, future—then static space, in
which changes of state occur, must be added as a fourth term.
In both cases, the fourth represents an incommensurable
Other that is needed for their mutual determination." *The Collected Works of C.G. Jung.* Volume 9, Part 2, p. 252.

dimensions of space to be made manifest a fourth "alien" dimension is needed: time. The converse is true: past, present, and future need space. How convenient if we could somehow extend this and come up with an equation in which x number of miles traveled in y number of years must equal individuation to the power of z. Unfortunately, the only thing we can know, up front, about a person who has journeyed many years in time is that he or she is old; and the only thing we can know about a person who has journeyed far in space is the number of miles traveled; and no kaballistic juggling with the external elements of the equation can tell us anything about the internal elements of the traveler.

This too we can learn from Odysseus: He has traveled twenty years and many, many miles without affecting his "internal elements" to any great extent. As we have seen in the above paragraph, we expect more of such seasoned travelers. In Odysseus' case, however, ten of his twenty wandering years have been spent in laying siege to Troy, and eight of the remaining ten with one or another of two extremely attractive immortals. Why, then, should we expect him to have learned any lessons other than those of war or love?

And yet Odysseus will journey within, but not in his Homeric incarnation; his individuation must wait many hundreds of years, for a poet of the twentieth century, a poet therefore who speaks for an age interested more in the inner than the outer journey. Which is as it should be if our "ripening of time" is on schedule.

But that Homer's hero does not individuate is right for yet another reason: he is too young!

> Midway the journey of this life I was 'ware
> That I had strayed into a dark forest,
> And the right path appeared not anywhere.
> Ah, tongue cannot describe how it oppressed,
> This wood, so harsh, dismal and wild, that
> fear
> At thought of it strikes now into my breast
> (8, p. 3).

Dante Alighieri was born in 1265. Modern man, it seems, did not invent the midlife crisis.

In her essay "The Process of Individuation," Jungian analyst Marie-Louise von Franz cites the dreams of seven patients. Five are in their late forties, one is described as middle-aged, only one as young. In the same essay she writes:

> The actual process of individuation—the conscious coming-to-terms with one's own inner center (psychic nucleus) or Self—generally begins with a wounding of the personality and the suffering that accompanies it. This initial shock amounts to a sort of "call".
>
> . . .
>
> Or perhaps everything seems outwardly all right, but beneath the surface a person is suffering from a deadly boredom that makes everything seem meaningless and empty.
> (18, p. 166)

At the time of the slaying of the suitors, Odysseus is approaching middle age, rather than already there. And the past twenty years, though they may have had their boring moments (sitting on the beach waiting to be summoned to Calypso's boudoir?) have hardly been such as would induce a state of ennui. Nor is there any evidence to suggest that his personality may have been wounded seriously enough for the individuation process to "self-start." He has experienced no initial shock; if he has heard a call it has been familiar—an old friend summoning him either to battle, deceit, or a beautiful woman.

But if Jungian psychology, and therefore individuation, is for the middle-aged (and this is not the place to enter into that discussion), no such problem exists with Self-realization. When reincarnation enters the picture, life assumes new and broader dimensions. If it is possible to be a high lama at the age of seven, it must be possible to be a Self-realized master at the age of six—but it will not be as a lama, high or low, that Odysseus reincarnates.

4

The Hero in Grey Flannel
(James Joyce, *Ulysses*)

This is the word of Lachesis, Daughter of Necessity. Souls of a day, here you must begin another round of mortal life. No Guardian Angel will be allotted to you; you shall choose your own.

. . .

And to see the souls choosing their lives was indeed a sight. . . . For the most part they followed the habits of their former life.

. . .

And so it happened that it fell to the soul of Odysseus to choose last of all. The memory of his former sufferings had cured him of all ambition and he looked round for a long time to find the uneventful life of an ordinary man; at last he found it lying neglected by the others, and when he saw it he chose it with joy and said that had his lot fallen first he would have made the same choice.

Plato, The Republic

Writing some six hundred years before the birth of Jesus, Plato tells us that for his next incarnation Odysseus has, with joy, chosen the life of an ordinary man. Meaning no disrespect to our reincarnating hero, one can well understand why none of his companions were anxious to contest his right to be reborn as Leopold Bloom.

Who is Leopold Bloom? When is Bloomsday? And why? What is *Ulysses*? And finally, why does this book and this face of the hero insist on its place in our thesis? In an essay entitled ''News of

33

The Joyce Industry,'' Father Thomas Merton gives us an idea of how difficult these questions are to answer:

> The mature critic recognizes that, in a work of such richness and complexity as Joyce's, one must not try to pin down, categorize, label, define, explain, classify, and prescribe. The art of Joyce is always rich in suggestion and in open possibilities, in delicate tensions, contrasts, unresolved problems that are not meant to be reduced to definite certainties. The stasis of the Joycean aesthetic is not a full stop in inertia, an end of living contradictions, but a delicate balance between them. (23)

So must we try neither to define nor to explain? If Father Merton does nothing else, he points out the dangers of plunging unprepared into the ''stasis of the Joycean aesthetic.''

C.G. Jung further underlines the difficulties awaiting the unwary reader.

> I started to read the book backwards. This method proved as good as the usual one; the book can just as well be read backwards, for it has no back and no front, no top and no bottom (17, p. 111).

It is instructive to compare the above comments. It is apparent that Merton, himself no mental slouch, was in awe of *Ulysses.* If he loved the book, he did so almost as one loves a god. Perhaps as a writer he realized that Joyce had set a

standard to which he himself could never hope to
aspire, indeed a standard so high that he was content merely to worship at the shrine, and en-
courage others to do the same. As we shall see,
this was not an isolated phenomenon: a generation
of intellectual artists were forever urging the
world, and each other, to "discover" James Joyce.

For C. G. Jung, on the other hand, there would
be no worshipping at the shrine. As we shall see,
his views softened somewhat with time, but it
seems safe to say that his main interest was never
so much with this "backless, frontless, topless,
bottomless" book as with the fascination it exerted
on so many readers. Thomas Merton's was not a
lone voice.

It is this question which must interest us. If
Ulysses insists on its place in our thesis—and it
does—why does it? And why did so many readers
accord this particular novel a kind of instant
apotheosis? To answer these questions we shall
have, once again, to consider ripeness and time.
But before doing that we must have some understanding of the phenomenon with which we are
dealing, and some idea of what this book is actually about. The material is complex; we must
approach it carefully. I'm sure the shade of Joyce
will forgive us if we take a figurative leaf from this
book and adopt as our format a kind of transmogrified catechism:

"Who is Leopold Bloom?"

"As a concrete particular he is a middle-aged advertisement-canvasser living in Dublin at the turn of the century."

"And in less concrete terms?"

"Ah. Well, he is probably that most ordinary of men whose life Odysseus chose as his next. Most critics agree that Bloom is Odysseus and Stephen Dedalus is Telemachus."

"Just a minute, exactly *who* is Stephen Dedalus?"

"As a concrete particular, he is a young man who is currently making a living as a school teacher. Most critics agree that Stephen is a self-portrait of James Joyce—the young Joyce of course. We first met Stephen in *Portrait of The Artist as A Young Man*—well, actually in *Stephen Hero.* You see in order even to begin to understand *Ulysses*, you must have read the *Portrait*, in fact *Ulysses* is full of references to characters in a book of short stories called *The Dubliners* and..."

"What about Bloomsday? When is it?"

"The sixteenth of June, 1904. This is one of the few things about which all critics agree."

"Very well, but *why* is Bloomsday? And you keep mentioning critics—why is that?"

"That's part of the answer to 'why is Bloomsday?' There are so many critics and commentators.

36

The very title of Father Merton's essay points this out: 'Notes From The Joyce Industry.' And that's what it is, an academic industry—writing about Ulysses. To many people *Ulysses* is, quite simply, the greatest, most important piece of literature of all time, so important that they celebrate the day on which all the action of the book takes place.''

''Very well. What is Ulysses?''

''As a concrete particular it's obviously a book. A thickish book written by James Joyce between the years 1914 and 1921 in Trieste, Zurich, and Paris. As a non-concrete whatever...well, whole volumes have been written about each of the principal characters, about each of the eighteen chapters, about the Odyssean parallels. To those who love it, it ranks with the word of God; to those who love it not, it's not a book but a crossword puzzle, a labyrinth of references and cross-references and counter-references, of Ariadne threads which may or may not lead to escape. It cannot be ignored.''

''It cannot be ignored, eh? Is that why it insists on its place in our thesis?''

Perhaps at this point it would be helpful to leave our catechism and briefly synopsize the book itself.

The action of *Ulysses* is set in the city of Dublin and takes place in a twenty-four-hour period. In that time its protagonists, Mr. Leopold Bloom, middle-aged advertisement canvasser, his wife Molly, and Stephen Dedalus, a young schoolteacher, will go about the everyday business of living.

Mr. Bloom will try to sell advertising space. He will receive a letter from a young lady who has never seen him, and knows him only as the mysterious Henry Flower. He will obtain an erotic novel for his wife, attend a funeral, and be the object of an anti-Semitic attack. Throughout the day he will try, unsuccessfully, to expel from his mind thoughts of the adultery his wife will consummate that afternoon with one Blazes Boylan. But for a while at least in the early evening, thoughts of his wife's infidelity will give way to fantasies of a more personal nature, as he gazes at young Gerty Macdowell sitting spread-legged on the rocks along Sandymount shore. Later that evening, his path and that of Stephen Dedalus, which have come close to crossing all day, will finally meet; and Bloom, sensing that the somewhat inebriated young man needs help, will act the guardian angel.

Stephen Dedalus, too, has been about a not unusual daily routine. He has risen at the same time as Bloom, taught school, collected his salary, run an errand for his headmaster, and discoursed on his personal theory of Hamlet and William Shakespeare; during the course of the day he has come increasingly to focus on his own dissatisfaction with his friends, his profession, his family, his very life.

Stephen and Leopold Bloom will visit a brothel; thereafter, the former having squandered most of his salary on rounds of drinks, and having been tricked into parting with the key to his home, will be taken to spend the night at the home of the latter. The book ends with the famous "Monologue of Molly Bloom," in which, lying in her bed, half awake, half asleep, Molly Bloom fantasizes, among other things, about having sex with the young man now visiting with her husband.

To get some idea of the difficulties involved in coming to terms with this book, consider the following: in his essay "The Empirical Molly," (32) David Hayman concludes that not only is Mrs. Bloom not a practiced adulteress, but that Blazes Boylan represents her first affair. However in "Some Determinants of Molly Bloom," (32) which appears in the same selection of essays, Darcy O'Brien concludes that in the matter of adultery Molly Bloom is a veritable daughter of Tyndareus.[1] There are three certainties here: 1) Both men cannot be right. 2) Each man strongly believes that he is right. 3) Since James Joyce is no longer with us, it is impossible to prove either man right—if indeed Joyce himself knew the answer, for in the universe which he created all answers are not only possible, but defensible.

"All men should 'unite to give praise to *Ulysses'*; those who will not may content themselves with a place in the lower intellectual orders." (29, p. 403) These words were written by Ezra Pound. As we

---

[1]Once, on sacrificing to the gods, Tyndareus overlooked Aphrodite. By way of revenge she swore to make all three of his daughters, Clytaemnestra, Timandra and Helen, notorious for their adulterous adventures.

have seen, he reflected the views of most, but not quite all, intellectuals of the day: "I had already taken up *Ulysses* in 1922 but had laid it aside disappointed and vexed. Today it still bores me as it did then" (17, p. 115).

With due respect to Ezra Pound, I doubt that even the most fanatical of Freudians would attempt to consign Carl Gustav Jung to "the lower intellectual orders." Since our thesis concerns individuation, and since individuation is a Jungian process, perhaps Jung's *"Ulysses: A Monologue,"* can, if not answer our final question, at least act as a signpost pointing to that answer.

> The only thing beyond dispute is that *Ulysses* is a book that has gone through ten printings and that its author is glorified by some and damned by others. He stands in the cross-fire of discussion and is thus a phenomenon which the psychologist should not ignore. Joyce has exerted a very considerable influence on his contemporaries, and it was this fact which first aroused my interest in *Ulysses*. Had this book slipped noiselessly and unsung into the shades of oblivion I would certainly never have dragged it back again; for it annoyed me thoroughly and amused me only a little. (17, p. 115)

It must have annoyed Jung very thoroughly indeed: in the course of twenty-three pages Jung mentions the 735 pages in his edition of *Ulysses* no less than seven times. For example:

> *Ulysses* is a book that pours along for seven hundred and thirty-five pages, a stream of time seven hundred and thirty-five days long which

all consist in one single and senseless day in the life of every man, the completely irrelevant sixteenth day of June, 1904, in Dublin—a day on which, in all truth, nothing happens (17, p. 109).

. . .

So far as I can see there are in those seven hundred and thirty-five pages no obvious repetitions, not a single blessed island where the long suffering reader may come to rest (17, p. 110).

. . .

The seven hundred and thirty-five pages that contain nothing by no means consist of blank paper but are closely printed. You read and read and read and you pretend to understand what you read....I read to page 135 with despair in my heart, falling asleep twice on the way (17, p. 110-11).

. . .

At the very end, or nearly the final page, a redeeming light breaks wistfully through the clouds. This is only *one* page against seven hundred and thirty-four which were one and all born of Orcus (17, p. 120).

What kind of anxiously guarded secret might it be that is hidden with matchless care under seven hundred and thirty-five unendurable pages? (17, p. 124)

When he mentions the seven hundred and thirty-five pages for the last time, Jung gives us some clue as to the meaning, or one of the meanings, that this book has for him:

It wants to be an eye of the moon, a consciousness detached from the object, in thrall neither to the Gods nor to sensuality, and

41

> bound neither by love nor by hate, neither by
> conviction nor by prejudice. *Ulysses* does not
> preach this but practices it—detachment of con-
> sciousness; and it is revealed not to him who
> has conscientiously waded through the seven
> hundred and thirty-five pages, but to him who
> has gazed at his world and his own mind for
> seven hundred and thirty-five days with the
> eyes of Ulysses. (17, p. 124)

Jung concludes that James Joyce's novel is a success because its "detachment of consciousness"
serves as an antidote to the "medieval sentimen-
tality" which permeates too many layers of the
Western world.

He further concludes that the Ulysses of the title,
and therefore Odysseus, refers not to Leopold
Bloom or any one character, but to the book itself,
and every character in the book, and every street
corner, and every scrap of paper—and to James
Joyce himself.

So what did Jung *really* think of those 735 unendurable pages—pages that bored him and were forever putting him to sleep? I believe that there is no
definite answer—there seem to be no definite
answers to anything concerning this book; but the
following letter, addressed to James Joyce and
signed by C.G. Jung, might bring us a step closer
to understanding—that is, if it doesn't take us two
steps further away:

> Dear Sir,
>   Your *Ulysses* has presented the world with
> such an unsettling psychological problem that

repeatedly I have been called in as a supposed authority on psychological matters.

. . .

Your book as a whole has given me no end of trouble and I was brooding over it for about three years until I succeeded in putting myself into it. But I must tell you that I'm profoundly grateful to yourself as well as to your gigantic opus, because I learned a great deal from it.

. . .

The 40 pages of non-stop run in the end is a string of veritable psychological peaches. I suppose the devil's grandmother knows so much about the real psychology of a woman, I didn't.

You may gather from my article what *Ulysses* has done to a supposedly balanced psychologist.

With the expression of my deepest appreciation, I remain, dear Sir,

Yours etc. (17, p. 133-34)

Jung, the inventor, discoverer—creator if you will—of individuation is ambivalent about *Ulysses:* on the one hand it puts him to sleep, on the other there are those "psychological peaches." This is not to say that he considers *Ulysses* a psychological novel, which indeed it is not, certainly not in the sense of *The Brothers Karamazov* or any of the wisdom tales woven by mythographers of old. But there is a paradox here, which is as it should be when considering *Ulysses;* while this is not, in the accepted sense, a psychological novel, it is chockfull of psychology. Joyce does not merely familiarize us with the physical shapes of his characters, he takes us inside their skin—inside their psyches—bares their souls. He shows us, not that 'psychology' which would manifest through their personas, but their inner psychology—the absolute truth of their being. We know these characters better than they know themselves, in truth better than they could know themselves, for the pain of such absolute self-knowledge would be too much for most to bear.

Joyce does more than provide us with absolute psychological insight into his characters; many writers have achieved as much, many more have attempted it. Joyce takes us into the rivers and streets and walls and cobblestones and scraps of paper of the city itself. He presents us, if you will, with the psychology of the city; and that city is not Dublin, it is every twentieth-century city; its people are not Dubliners, they are twentieth-century man. They are you and I. In this sense it is possible to see Dublin as the precursor of Stan Freberg's "grey-flannel nightmare," and Leopold Bloom as the spiritual father of that unfortunate creature who was a perfectly respectable werewolf by night, but by day a "grey-flannel something" came over him and he turned into—an Advertising Man!

At this stage it is necessary for us to digress and attempt to place Jung in some sort of time frame. In a conversation, Stephan Hoeller[2] pointed out to me the perhaps surprising similarities between Jung and H.P. Blavatsky, whose magnum opus *The*

---

[2]Dr. Hoeller is the author of *The Royal Road* and *The Gnostic Jung and The Seven Sermons to The Dead*, both published by Quest.

Secret Doctrine is the foundation of modern theosophy. The significant points are that, broadly speaking, they occupy the same historical epoch; and that, though the emphasis was different for each, they both stated that man could be *more*. Not insignificantly, within the same time frame Nietzsche was saying much the same thing:

> Behold, I teach you the overman.
>
> . . .
>
> Man is a rope tied between beast and over-man—a rope over an abyss.
>
> . . .
>
> What is great in man is that he is a bridge and not an end. (27, p. 14-15)

To open the Nietzschean can of worms would be to expand this work to an untenable length. What is important is to realize the number of heralds who were saying approximately the same thing at approximately the same time, that therefore perhaps the time was ripe for whatever the message—or rather messages—had to say.

This is not the place to discuss in depth the modern city and its effect on modern man. But in order to understand this face of the hero, we must acknowledge that the modern city and its con-comitant technology have greatly increased man's material comfort and physical well-being, though they have done nothing for his spirit, for his psychology, if you will. As modern man's leisure time has increased, so has his inner emptiness. Commentators representing a dozen disciplines have made this point ad nauseam and are making it still. I have no intention of joining their ranks except to point out the almost synchronistic arrival, not merely of psychology, which might ease the pain of modern man, but of heralds of the human spirit, who told man that, yes, there is more—and he could be more.

We have moved closer to answering our final question, which, lest we forget, was: "Why does *Ulysses* insist on 'its place in our thesis?' " For the final clue let us turn from sages, psychologists, and academic "isms" to a more worldly, nay more earthy, wisdom, that of Henry Miller:

> If *The Odyssey* is a remembrance of great deeds, *Ulysses* is a forgetting...The story of Ulysses is the story of a lost hero recounting a lost myth....The great Homeric figure of Ulysses, shrunk to the insignificant shadow, now of Bloom, now of Dedalus, wanders through the dead and forsaken world of the big city; the anemic, distorted and desiccated reflections of what were once epic events.
>
> .   .   .
>
> Joyce reveals the desperate plight of the modern man who, lashing about in his steel and concrete cage, admits finally that there is no way out.
>
> .   .   .
>
> Ulysses is a paean to "the late-city man," a thanatopsis inspired by the ugly tomb in which the soul of the civilized man lies embalmed. (24)

Thanatopsis. That one word sums up all that Henry Miller has to say about *Ulysses*. "Thanatopsis'' means a contemplation of death. For Henry Miller then, *Ulysses* is not about a coming to terms with late-city life, but an acceptance that, for Joyce, his protagonists—and how many others?—late-city life is little more than a contemplation of death, a mere existence, a protracted awaiting of a preordained end.

For such as these there is no overman; their greatest outer odyssey two weeks at the seaside, their journey within either anger at this emptiness or a wistful awareness that there must be more than this!

Perhaps neither the opinion of C. G. Jung nor of Henry Miller should surprise us. With the exception of Molly Bloom's soliloquy, which he regarded as a penetrating insight into the psyche of women, Jung was thoroughly bored by the book. This reaction obviously violated the expectations of the publisher who asked for his opinion; but should it have? The bulk of Jung's life work was concerned with individuation, with showing man that he could be more—saying, in effect, that yes, overman exists and man could be overman. Surely it's not hard to picture such a man being bored by a book which a near contemporary could describe as a thanatopsis?

What of that near contemporary, Henry Miller? He is best remembered as the man who wrote *Tropic of Cancer* and *Tropic of Capricorn,* to say nothing of *The Rosy Crucifixion*—"dirty" books which were printed in Paris and, until the nine-

47

teen-sixties, had to be smuggled into the English-speaking world. But whatever else the books may have been, they were full of humor and earthy wisdom, a love of life and a passion for living.

In the early 1940s the expatriate returned from France and traveled extensively in America, the land of his birth. The result was *The Air-Conditioned Nightmare*. The book dwelt on the cost in human terms of mechanization and commercialization. The title pretty well sums up Miller's feelings; for whatever he may have felt about individuation, or Self-realization, or inner and outer odysseys, he believed that life, everyday life, day-to-day life, should be made to yield to the living every last drop, not merely of pleasure, but of *everything*. It was by this standard that he lived his own life, by this standard too that he judged *Ulysses*. By this standard he saw what it was not, therefore saw also what it was—and named it "Thanatopsis."

To accept Miller's description as being at least partially accurate is to come a long way, not only toward answering our question, but also to understanding the wide fascination of *Ulysses*.

Leopold Bloom, advertisement-canvasser, twentieth-century man in his twentieth-century city—grey flannel nightmare. His may not be the face of a hero as heroes are commonly understood, but his is the face of our time—a survivor clothing himself with as much dignity as is available. Perhaps, in our time, even this much is not un-heroic.

It is because *Ulysses* is the finest portrait yet painted, in any medium, of late-city and late-city dwellers that it demands its place in our thesis. And surely this, as much as the pyrotechnical brilliance of Joyce's technique, explains the enduring fascination of this work. For better or worse, we can in its Dublin see at least some part of our city, and in its characters at least some part of ourselves.

But the age of Ulysses has also been an age of heralds; for heralds come when they are most needed. This was, and is, their message: man is not an end, but a bridge; he can individuate; he can journey within; he can be *more*.

And so, once again, our hero will reincarnate. Paradoxically, he will travel backwards and forwards at the same time: backwards in physical time to an heroic material world, forwards in Psyche's time to an heroic spiritual world. Now his odyssey will be not merely without, but within; and twentieth-century man—Leopold Bloom if you will, hungry for meaning, for hope—will watch, and so, perhaps, better understand the message of the heralds.

5

A Handbook for the Future
(Nikos Kazantzakis, "The Odyssey, A Modern Sequel")

Odysseus sealed his bitter lips and spoke no more,
but watched the glowering fire fade, the withering
  flames,
the ash that spread like powder on the dying coals,
then turned, glanced at his wife, gazed on his son
  and father,
and suddenly shook with fear, and sighed, for now
  he knew
that even his native land was a sweet mask of Death.
Like a wild beast snared in a net, his eyes rolled
  round
and tumbled down his deep eye-sockets, green and
  bloodshot.
His tribal palace seemed a narrow shepherd's pen,
his wife a small and wrinkled old housekeeping crone,
his son an eighty-year-old drudge.
                              .   .   .
He turned and looked about him: all his streets
  seemed narrow.
                        .   .
The foxy-minded man then laughed till the earth
  shook:
"Strange fruits are sweetest and strange breasts smell
  best of all!
O Rotting hull, my native land, you rise and fall
between my brows and break on the mind's jagged
  cliffs!"
                        .   .   .
...but sorrow crushed the manly chest of the
  world-traveler
for he recalled how when waves tore his prow he
  longed
to reach his rocky isle and to hold council here
under this plane-tree grove with his town elders
  round him—
was this, by God, the foul fistful his soul desired?
                              Nikos Kazantzakis

50

Odysseus' twenty-year dream is over: he has come home to Ithaca, and he wishes he hadn't arrived. And, in truth, he hasn't—and he never can; for if, as Thomas Wolfe pointed out, "You can't go home again," that is because there is no home to go to. To the man who travels far in time, home is not merely another place, but another day—yesterday. Odysseus' Ithaca is twenty years of yesterdays away.

"I did not recognize what my own people had become and they did not recognize me" (34, p. 273). Thus wrote Sir Laurens van der Post on returning, after an absence of many years, to his native South Africa. How accurately these words describe Odysseus' situation! Like van der Post, he has come home; like van der Post, he must look, not at subjective yesterday, but at objective today. In Odysseus' case his soul screams—a scream born not merely of present disappointment, but of a presentiment of boredom to come—and boredom, we may recall, is one of the heralds, if not of individuation, then at least of the possibility of individuation.

Before traveling any further, let us stop and speculate. What would have happened if Palamedes had not seen through Odysseus' play-acting? We can never know what our protagonist would be like if he had never left Ithaca, but we may speculate.

> In a sweet stupor, drugged with so much food
>   and drink,
> fat Menelaus watched with heavy-lidded eyes
>   (19, p. 96).

It seems reasonable to suppose that, given similar life-paths, Menelaus and Odysseus might be not unalike. Both have been warriors; both are wealthy; both are monarchs; both have beautiful wives; both are middle-aged, or approaching middle age. Both therefore are ready for that greater or lesser metanoia which our epoch has labelled "the midlife crisis." Both are ripe, or could be ripe, for individuation. Yet one is physically lean and mentally hungry and the other "in a sweet stupor."

And what of the women? Anima figures are of prime importance in any study which, however obliquely, concerns itself with individuation; and one of the women, Helen of Sparta—of Troy and again of Sparta—enjoys the status of an archetype. She fits into Marie-Louise von Franz's hierarchy of anima figures:

> The number four is also connected with the anima because, as Jung noted, there are four stages to its development. The first stage is best symbolized by Eve, which represents purely instinctual and biological relations. The second can be seen in Faust's Helen: She personifies a romantic and aesthetic level that is, however, still characterized by sexual elements. The third is represented, for instance, by the Virgin Mary—a figure who raises love (eros) to the heights of spiritual devotion. The fourth type is symbolized by Sapienta, wisdom transcending even the most holy and the most pure. (18, p. 185)

The fact that that esoteric lady, Sapienta, is less than a household word hardly matters—as wisdom anima she represents a very rarely attained stage of development. Perhaps not that many attain the third stage, but enough do it to make it important that the lady chosen to symbolize that stage be instantly recognizable. The Virgin Mary certainly qualifies, as does Eve in the position of the most frequently met of all anima figures.

That Helen of Troy should have been chosen to represent the stage of anima development which comes between Eva and Mary is an indication of how ''recognizable'' a lady she is. The average citizen might have trouble identifying Prometheus as the thief of fire, or even Zeus as the king of gods, but ask him whose face it was that ''launched a thousand ships,'' and there is an excellent chance of seeing a smile, and hearing, ''Oh, that was Helen of Troy.''

Furthermore, Helen is forever reincarnating—she appears in the literature of the Gnostics as the companion of Simon Magus: ''Helen was the human soul fallen into matter and Simon the mind which brings about her redemption'' (22, p. 168). Penelope and Helen. Their circumstances are as similar as their husbands, and yet

> as she waited by the throne in pallid,
>   speechless dread
> Penelope turned to look, and her knees shook
>   with fright:
>   ''That's not the man I've awaited year on
>   year, O Gods,
> This forty-footed dragon that stalks my quak-
>   ing house!'' (19, p. 3)

What of Helen?

> And Helen, bent above her golden cup,
>   rejoiced
> in his dread glance, abandoned to his rude
>   caresses (19, p. 96).

Penelope has been without husband or lover for twenty years, but it seems that the husband she wanted was complacent Menelaus. Helen has never been without either husband or lover—or both; and for the ten years since the end of the Trojan war, that husband/lover has been complacent Menelaus—but Helen wants the non-complacent Odysseus.

This is not mere greener-grassism, nor is it idle speculation. Perhaps, like Kazantzakis' *Odysseus*, we live between eras. Perhaps not. But certainly we live in an interesting age; as dwellers in such an age, should we not remember the Chinese curse: "May you be born in an interesting age"?

Music reflects its epoch; painting reflects its epoch; all art which is art reflects its epoch. But surely no art reflects better than literature, and surely none can better help us to understand, and in an epoch as interesting as ours, is it not important, even essential, to at least try to understand?

Odysseus and Helen are our most enduring literary archetypes. Odysseus may be transmogrified as Leopold Bloom; Helen may be cast as a mere whore—but they endure. They are as alive in our century as they were in Homer's. And ours, more than any other, is the century of psychology, of individuation, of awareness of Self-realization— and mass self-destruction. For every complacent twentieth-century Menelaus, there are how many twentieth-century screaming-souled Odysseuses?

Before attempting to answer this question, or examining the changing faces of this particular hero, we must consider, not only the Kazantzakis poem, but the act of creation which produced it. And here we must be careful; "The Odyssey, A Modern Sequel" is very, very long, and very, very complex:

> [It] is one of the great encyclopaedic works of our time, encompassing the major motifs of our civilization and Homer's (20, p. 115).
>
> . . .
>
> Its union of metaphysics and gross sensuality, its function as an encyclopaedia of modernist thought (20, p. 113).
>
> . . .
>
> . . . may well turn out to be the spiritual hand- book of the future . . . our future may well lie within its pages (9, p. 29).

Vis-a-vis the first of the above quotes—no one who had read Kazantzakis' poem would deny that it is one of "the great encyclopaedic works of our time"; and certainly, to introduce the second quote, metaphysics and sensuality are major motifs of our time. This was also true in Homer's time, and seems bound to continue to be true through foreseeable tomorrows. In which case, to introduce the third quote, this book has at least the potential to be the spiritual handbook of the next thousand years or so. There is, after all, some precedent for this: how many years ago were most of today's spiritual handbooks written?

Fortunately, the briefest of synopses will serve our purpose—with an underlining of those aspects of this "spiritual handbook of the future" that directly affect our argument: Odysseus, bored with Ithaca, decides to leave. He assembles a crew: Captain Clam, a trustworthy old man of the sea; Kentaur, a food-loving bon vivant; Orpheus, a poet and mystic seeker; Hardihood, a burly bronzesmith from the mountains; Granite, who killed his brother in a fight over a woman; and the shepherd Rocky, who will join them in Sparta. In "The Cretan Glance" Morton P. Levitt suggests that, while Captain Clam, Kentaur, and Orpheus symbolize all too human qualities which Odysseus will have to surpass, Hardihood, Granite, and Rocky represent historical forces beyond nature which Odysseus must move beyond. While this is no more than we should expect from a "spiritual handbook of the future" I believe that, in one way or another, all six characters represent aspects of Odysseus himself—aspects which he will trans-cend, outgrow, leave behind—as he journeys from Ithaca to the South Pole.

Our hero's first port of call is Sparta. He is drawn there, not by friendship for Menelaus, but by memories of Helen; and Helen, as bored as was

Odysseus and for the same reasons, is only too happy to be abducted.

As the archetypal personification of the second stage of anima development, Helen, ''personifies a romantic and aesthetic level that is, however, still characterized by sexual elements.'' At this stage of his twin journeys, it is safe to say that Odysseus is never unaware of sexual elements; however, ''he considers how Helen has never been for him a carnal temptation, but has always inspired him to the high valor of the mind'' (19, p. 780).

A frightened Menelaus has given ''blond barbarians'' permission to settle in Sparta. Kinsmen of these same barbarians invade Crete. Odysseus fights with them to overthrow a land grown effete under the weight of its own civilization; for he sees the need for new blood, understands the paradox that only by an infusion of the *un*civilized can civilization itself survive. Odysseus proclaims Hardihood the new King; and Helen, impregnated by a blond gardener, also remains on Crete.

From Crete to Egypt. Once again, Odysseus sides with those seeking to overthrow a decadent regime. This time he is unsuccessful. Pharaoh's guards escort Odysseus and his troop from the land.

And so the odyssey continues, through Africa to the source of the Nile; through conversations with God to the building, and subsequent destruction, of an ideal city; through becoming an ascetic to meetings with figures symbolic, among others, of Christ and Buddha. And on, on to the South Pole and:

> All the great body of the world-roamer turned to mist
> and slowly his snow-ship, his memory, fruit, and friends
> drifted like fog far down the sea, vanished like dew.
> The flesh dissolved, glances congealed, the heart's pulse stopped,
> and the great mind leapt to the peak of its holy freedom,
> fluttered with empty wings, then upright through the air
> soared high and freed itself from its last cage, its freedom.
> All things like frail mist scattered till but one brave cry
> for a brief moment hung in the calm benighted waters:
> "Forward, my lads, sail on, for Death's breeze blows in a fair wind." (19, p. 775)

The poem has ended. Odysseus' long voyages are over, both the voyage within, and the voyage without—at least in terms understandable to men still mortal. For who among us dare speculate as to what voyages might lie ahead for the great mind—spirit if you will—of our most enduring hero. He might have journeyed on, might be journeying still, to nirvanas beyond the perception of earth-bound eyes. But if he has journeyed beyond individuation, he has also journeyed *through* individuation: at some stage he reached the plateau that is, for most of us, the terminus of our inner journey. A broad terminus certainly, and one that will take much exploring, but a terminus none the less.

It would be ridiculous to dissect line by line, even chapter by chapter, a very difficult, very long poem in an attempt to pinpoint the exact moment at which the hero of the poem can be said to have individuated. Surely what matters is not *when* Odysseus individuated, but that he *did* individuate, and that however exotic, however fantastic, the path chosen for his particular feet by the gods of fate and karma, its twists and turns and stopping places are basically the same as those on all paths leading to individuation.

Our hero accepts and integrates all aspects of himself. These aspects are like an ascending ladder: he comes to terms not with one shadow figure, but with all shadows. Perhaps there is only one anima but if there is, then Odysseus must come to terms with all aspects of that anima. And still the ladder stretches before him—now there are figures of the Self, of Jesus and Buddha.

Is there an end to individuation—or to Self-realization? Is there, as implied above, a final terminus? Perhaps some anthropomorphic God, or a projected image of Self, who waits to pat us on the back: "Well done. You made it. Now you're the best you can possibly be—for this life anyway." For most of humankind, some less fanciful version of the above is probably true. Not of course that there is an actual terminus—an Ultima Thule beyond which merely human aspirations may not stretch—but that the journey is long and the terminus, which is individuation, is very large. It must be explored. It must be fully understood. The Self-realized must remain Self-realized. But, then, can the truly Self-realized ever again be *un*Self-realized?

It's all too easy to lose one's way in questions such as this. Constructing a metaphysical Möbius strip is simple; the hard thing is not to return again and again to the same point. And yet there is a clue, a hint as to, if not *the* answer, at least *an* answer. Odysseus, the forever traveler, the forever runner-towards, is not prepared to stop at individuation or Self-realization. His ladder still ascends before him. He moves on—upward. But now he no longer climbs, for he no longer has to. His material body no longer exists. He is spirit. That spirit is journeying still, though perhaps not even the poet himself knows in what realms it now travels. Perhaps then, for us humans, while yet made of matter, our imaginary terminus is terminus indeed. A symbolic or actual point marking a realization of potential beyond which matter cannot travel.

6

The Hero in Limbo

I saw the best minds of my generation destroyed by
madness,
  Starving hysterical naked
dragging themselves through the negro streets at
dawn looking for
  an angry fix,
angelheaded hipsters burning for the ancient heavenly
connection
  to the starry dynamo in the machinery of night...
                              Allen Ginsberg, "Howl"

Nikos Kazantzakis commenced writing his Odyssey
on Crete in September of 1924. He was almost
forty-two years old. According to his biographer,
Pandelis Prevelakis, he had not yet decided on his
own destiny (30, p. 110).

"The Odyssey: A Modern Sequel" was revised
seven times; it is written in twenty-four books; it
contains 33,333 lines; its first printing, which was
private, consisted of exactly three-hundred copies;
it took Kazantzakis fourteen years to complete.
These facts are not idly presented. They must be
considered if we are to understand the act of creation mentioned in the previous chapter.

It is not for us to judge whether or not Nikos
Kazantzakis ever achieved individuation or, for
that matter, Self-realization, nor is this important.

What is important is that at forty-two years of age
the poet must have been approximately the same
age as his hero; and Prevelakis has pointed out
how much poet and hero are one. Kazantzakis is a
constant traveler, a constant seeker without and
within; but often the seeker within Kazantzakis is
Odysseus—and vice versa. And forty-two, or
thereabouts, is a good age for midlife crisis, for
new beginnings, for journeys which, though their
termini may never be reached or seen or even
understood, are for some ineluctable.

Kazantzakis' poem did not simply "happen" to
require seven revisions, any more than it simply
happened to divide itself into twenty-four books.
There is one book for every letter of the Greek
alphabet, and even before starting to write,
Kazantzakis planned seven revisions, for seven has
long been a number of completion:

> Seven: Symbolic of perfect order, a complete
> period or cycle. It comprises the union of the
> ternary and the quaternary, and hence it is en-
> dowed with exceptional value. It corresponds
> to the seven directions of space (that is, the six
> existential directions plus the center), to the
> seven-pointed star, to the reconciliation of the
> square with the triangle by superimposing the
> latter upon the former (as the sky over the
> earth) or by inscribing it within. It is the num-
> ber forming the basic series of musical notes,
> of colors and of the planetary spheres, as well
> as of the gods corresponding to them; and also
> of the capital sins and their opposing virtues. It
> also corresponds to the three-dimensional

62

cross, and, finally, it is the symbol of pain.
(6, p. 233)

This definition is taken from J.E. Cirlot's *A Dictionary of Symbols,* but to Kazantzakis such things were not mere symbols—not, at any rate, as most of us understand symbols. Perhaps we can get some conception of the importance which Kazantzakis attached to such things by reading his own explanation of the importance—the *necessity*—of his "Odyssey" consisting of 33,333 lines, and of a first "special" printing of 300 copies:

> The number three is a holy number simply because it is the mathematical expression of the dialectical progression of the mind from thesis to antithesis and finally to the summit of every endeavour, synthesis. I can never think of an *A* without at the same time thinking of and accepting an *A-*, and to want at once, in order to free myself from this antinomy, to unite them both into a synthesis, into an *A+*. The *A* always seems to me a miserable thing, no matter how useful it may be in practical life; the *A-* seems to me scant and infertile, and only the *A+* succeeds in making firm, in fertilizing, and in disburdening my thought. This triple rhythm, transferred from dialectical thought into a metaphysical and mystical vision, gave birth to all the Holy Trinities in many religions. . . . In the case of "The Odyssey," however, it is not necessary to seek recourse to mysticism or orientalism; the number three is holy because it symbolizes the dialectical progression which the thought and diction of "The Odyssey" follow. (19, p. xxxv)

63

If, as seems safe to assume, Kazantzakis did not consciously plan to spend fourteen years in the writing of his masterwork, then perhaps Fate or the Muses combined with his unconscious. Some of the mystic properties of seven travel with all multiples of that number, and those attached to fourteen are particularly apt:

> Each septenary is really a fourteen, because each of the seven has its two aspects. Thus fourteen signifies the inter-relation of two planes in its turn (2, p. 522).
>
> . . .
>
> Fourteen: Stands for fusion and organization and also for justice and temperance (6, p. 234).

To the modern mind it may seem strange, even ridiculous, to associate temperance with either Kazantzakis or his "Odyssey." But the temperance we are speaking of is not that of the society which fought so hard against alcohol; it is that of the fourteenth card of the Tarot, where "its meaning is associated rather with the tempering of steel." (12, p. 66) How appropriate then that Kazantzakis should have "happened" to spend fourteen years writing his masterwork; for in those years was not the book tempered by the fire of the man, even as the man was tempered by the fire of life, even as steel is tempered by the fire of fire?

So we see that in this act of creation everything is charged with meaning: the physical dimensions of the poem—twenty-four books, 33,333 lines, 300 copies printed—and even the fourth dimension. Time has cooperated, has lent its meaning to the poem. "I wrote in the seventeen-syllable line because this followed more truly the rhythm of my blood when I lived the Odyssey." (19, p. XXVII) The book is the man; the man is the book. Within and without the man, whose main influences in life were Christ, Buddha, and Lenin, is a forever-traveler—forever seeking, forever growing, forever wanting more for man. And the book and its hero? The book is the man—the man is the book—the man is the hero.

Of the three archetypes who have, as it were, emerged from the womb of the master *archetype*—the master Odysseus—the first, Homer's hero, spans the greatest number of years, is the most prolific in terms of literary offspring, and is the easiest to understand. Perhaps we can better come to terms with the others if we examine them and their creators, not in isolation, but by means of comparing them to one another.

Nikos Kazantzakis was born in 1883; James Joyce in 1882. It is perhaps fair to say that the former was a constant traveler, the latter a constant expatriate. One can take this a step further and say that Kazantzakis was a constant seeker. He looked without, at man and the world; he looked within for an ideal which was "more"; thereafter he would strive, within and without, to realize that ideal. He was constantly seeking—constantly running *to*, rather than away. He was, as we have seen, forty-two years old when he started his "odyssey," and "had not yet decided his destiny."

James Joyce was thirty-two years old when he commenced work on his *Ulysses*. He had decided his destiny—he knew he was a writer. He too had looked without—at Ireland, specifically at Dublin. It seems fair to say that if Joyce did run to something it was primarily to escape from something else: Joyce ran *away* rather than *to*. But if life has a dictator, his name is Paradox, and James Joyce would be forever cathected to the very womb from which he had run. For the rest of his life he would probe that womb, the dust in the cracks in the cobble-stoned streets, the secret corners and hidden places in the minds of the people, their conscious thoughts, their unconscious urges, their very dreams.

Dreams of the day and dreams of the night. These play an important part in the writings of both men. It was said of Kazantzakis' hero:

> Odysseus dreams of fate in the form of a woman who stabs him with three knives, with three great experiences and adventures in life: woman in youth, war and glory in manhood, and death in old age (19, p. 786)
>
> . . .
>
> He creates various fantasies of his mind— nymphs, the twelve months, werewolves, creatures of myth and legend, and finally an image of God as a vain, bearded, staggering dwarf. . . . He destroys the image and rejoices in his own freedom. (19, p. 800)
>
> . . .
>
> A voice now cries out thrice within him, and Odysseus recognizes Heracles, his great fore-father who had struggled through twelve

labors to purify his spirit through flame into
light, who taught him to pass beyond all small
passions, to aim at the great, and to strive still
further, all in terms of actual deeds performed.
(19, p. 800).

Actual deeds performed. Compare this with Sandymount shore, with Mr. Leopold Bloom and the
spread-legged Miss Gertrude MacDowell. Compare
Odysseus' dream of a woman wielding three fate-
charged knives, his fantasies of nymphs, were-
wolves, and a dwarf god, with the sad, secret cor-
respondence of Bloom's *nom de guerre*, Henry
Flower; and with Molly Bloom, her erotic books
and fantasies. One is tempted to agree with that
commentator who suggested that Molly Bloom was
not, after all, a prolific adulteress. Perhaps Blazes
Boylan was the only "actual deed performed"—
perhaps, like her husband, she was merely a great
fantasizer.

German poet and dramatist Johann Schiller once
pointed out that it is possible to find the naive and
the sentimental not only in the same poet, but in
the same poem. We should bear this in mind
before allowing ourselves to play "psychoanalyzing
the writer." Joyce and Kazantzakis: Who was the
introvert? Who the extrovert? Who was Dionysian?
Who Apollonian? If we accept that Joseph Conrad
was correct when he said that the writer lives in
his work, then surely these are important questions. And surely answers, correct answers, must
bring us closer to understanding not only the faces
of the hero, but the forces which have molded
those faces.

At first glance it would seem that the correct answers to all these questions must be in the affirmative, and that first glance is probably correct. However a second glance might suggest that the differences between the writers in question—the "psychological" differences if you will—are so obvious that they hardly need to be examined, and that even were this not so, such an examination is not within the province of this book. Let us therefore assume, rightly or wrongly, that both Joyce and Kazantzakis achieved, in their work if not in their lives, the Nietzschean ideal of combined Apollonian and Dionysian characteristics. (26)

Furthermore, as fascinating as these distinctions may be, there is another which can bring us much closer to understanding our heroes and their message. Henry Miller's dubbing *Ulysses* as "Thanatopsis" gives us the clue. It is possible, even probable, that James Joyce/Ulysses and Nikos Kazantzakis/Odysseus see the same world and the same state of modern man—they see Limbo, a place of oblivion that is neither here nor there. Both run. Joyce runs away. But Limbo runs with him, and will live with him forever. Limbo-Ireland. Limbo-Dublin. Limbo-people, some of whom see their Limbo-streets and Limbo-houses and Limbo-lives. And they protest, but theirs are Limbo-protests: letters by Henry Flower and erotic novels. And they scream, but Limbo-screams are murmurs; and murmur multiplied by murmur is the sound of Limbo—of Thanatopsis.

Kazantzakis never runs away—he runs toward. Horrified by Limbo, he seeks non-Limbo. When he screams it is to defy the gods themselves, and we can well believe that the very stars hear him. He journeys within and without. He seeks more—and he becomes more—and he is not alone. Another poet, Allen Ginsberg, screams too:

> ...who lit cigarettes in boxcars boxcars boxcars racketing through snow
>   toward lonesome farms in grandfather night
>
>   .   .   .
>
> who loned it through the streets of Idaho seek-ing visionary indian
>   angels who were visionary indian angels
>
>   .   .   .
>
>   who lounged hungry and lonesome through Houston seeking jazz
>   or sex or soup, and followed the brilliant Spaniard to
>   converse about America and Eternity, a hopeless task, and so
>   took ship to Africa,
> who disappeared into the volcanoes of Mexico leaving behind
>   nothing but the shadow of dungarees and the lava and ash
>   of poetry scattered in fireplace Chicago
>   (10, p. 11)
>
>   .   .   .
>
> What sphinx of cement and aluminum bashed open their skulls
>   and ate up their brains and imagination?
> Moloch! Solitude! Filth! Ugliness! Ashcans and unobtainable dollars! Children screaming under the stairways! Boys
>   sobbing in armies! Old men weeping in the parks!
>
>   .   .   .
>
> Moloch whose eyes are a thousand blind windows!

> Moloch whose
>> skyscrapers stand in the long streets like
> endless Jehovahs!
>> Moloch whose factories dream and croak in
> the fog!
>> Moloch whose smokestacks and antennae
> crown the cities! (10, p. 17)

Allen Ginsberg's "Howl," whose metaphorical Moloch is first cousin to Miller's Thanatopsis, was first published in 1956; the English translation of Kazantzakis' "Odyssey" in 1957; and in the fifties over a dozen books came from the pen of one Jack Kerouac, among them *On The Road* and *San Francisco Blues.*

In the late fifties and early sixties the Beat Generation was called many things. A few felt threatened by it. A few distrusted it. Doubtless, a few even hated it. But most of the mainstream Western world were simply confused. If people sensed that all this might, just possibly, represent more than the usual generation gap, they still didn't understand what it was all about, any more than a decade earlier they had been able to understand Henry Miller's *Air Conditioned Nightmare.* (Of course his other books, like the *Tropics*, were different. They might have been dirty, but you could understand dirty!)

In truth how, at any time between the end of World War II and the beginning of all that which would come to be symbolized by Vietnam, could anyone who was not at least a little weird refer to America as a nightmare of any sort?

70

Again we are confronted with time and the ripeness of time; and again we must promise to return to this question. For the moment, the important thing to understand is that while this Beat Generation was born to enjoy the fruits of a land of milk and honey, it was hungry—not for food, but for meaning. Significantly, in terms of our theme, that meaning would be sought, not in the material richness of the West, but in the spiritual richness of the East.

There was nothing unique in this. Throughout history individuals and groups had done much the same thing. What distinguished this particular "turning to the East" was its relative spontaneity and its relative largeness. The voice of the Beats was not that of a small group who could be ignored, laughed at, or condescendingly tolerated, according to personal whim—this was the Beat *Generation*. As loud as the collective voice of this generation may have been in its own time, it was still soft in terms of time qua time—it might easily have disappeared and left no significant trace. But it did not. It was the voice of a true herald.

Ginsberg, Kerouac, Ferlinghetti, Snyder. The name Nikos Kazantzakis has never appeared on a list of Beat Generation luminaries; and yet, in one sense at least, he would be right at home, for these were, and are, all children of the third archetype, reincarnated from the master *archetype* which is Odysseus. All will see Moloch-Thanatopsis, all will scream, all will challenge the old gods, all will seek. Some will run away, but most will run

71

towards. Like Odysseus they will dream; perhaps they too will try to build the ideal city—if not in steel and stone, in heart and mind.

> Free *from* what? As if that mattered to Zarathustra! But your eyes should tell me brightly: free *for* what (27, p. 63).

This then was, and is, the third face of the Odyssean Hero, the face with eyes brightly answering: "For what? Why for more, if not to reach, at least to stretch towards?" As we have seen, the path which many—nay most—of these heroes will see as leading to that "more" will be paved with eastern concepts. Jack Kerouac also wrote *DHARMA Bums*, a book destined to become almost as popular as *On the Road* itself.

7

A Search for the Infinite
(Leo Tolstoy, *War and Peace*)

Tolstoy's subject is humanity—people moving in the strange delirium of war and war's chaos. The historic scenes are used as a foil and background for the personal dramas of those who took part in them.

Rosemary Edwards

Homer's Odysseus—hero and anti-hero. Archetypal source of a broad literary stream in whose waters swim pirates and private eyes, spies and space-adventurers. Leopold Bloom—neither hero nor anti-hero. Non-hero then. But he too an archetype; and from him will come others, grey flannel denizens of Thanatopsis; their achievement—their odyssey if you will—to live each day, to survive, or, like Arthur Miller's tragic salesman, not survive. And Kazantzakis' Odysseus. He too hero and anti-hero—even, perhaps, non-hero. His screams at once of pain and protest. His very life an Odyssey—a quest for the more meaningful. And this will be true of those who came with him, and who follow him, "Yackety-yacking through grandfather night."

For most of us, Odysseus, whether hero of Homer or Kazantzakis, is larger than life—larger, certainly, than our lives. In his earlier incarnation his derring-do may hugely entertain us; in his later incarnation we may understand his screams, may even dimly see his path, but most of us could no more follow that path than could Leopold Bloom. But not all journeys of individuation, in literature or in life itself, are on quite such an epic scale, or played out against so mythic a backdrop:

> When a human being has achieved some degree of self-awareness, he is able to make choices that are different from those of the flock and to express himself in ways that are uniquely his own....He will be free to act in ways that fulfill his deepest needs and express his truest self.
>
> It is important to note here that as a person gains the independence to be a nonconformist, he also gains the self-assurance to be a conformist. As Jung has often stressed, an individuated person is not the same as someone who is individualistic. He is not driven to conform to custom, but he is equally not driven to defy it. He does not try to set himself apart from his peers by affecting peculiar dress or by exhibiting outlandish behavior.
>
> . . .
>
> It is as if everything about him—his clothes, his gestures, his way of sitting or standing— belongs to him. Nothing about him is superimposed. Everything he says or does appears to arise from his deepest center. (25, p. 19)

What Sallie Nichols is attempting in the above paragraphs is to describe a fully individuated human being. That this is no easy task is shown by her near contradictions. At one moment this ideal person is neither driven to defy custom nor to set himself apart from his peers by adopting outlandish clothing; a moment later not only this

74

man's clothes, but his gestures and way of sitting
are unique. Surely, at any rate in the eyes of the
general public, such a man would have to be described as a non-conformist. Never mind that; a
few lines earlier, we have been told that he would
have the self-assurance to be a conformist.

Yet we all know what the writer means; it is
hard to describe an individuated person, one who
conforms, not merely to himself, but to his SELF.
Perhaps the best advice in the world, at once the
most repeated and the most ignored, is that of
Polonius to his son, Laertes, "to thine own self be
true" (31, p. 13). But this advice is not willfully
ignored—most of us would like nothing better than
to be true to what we perceive as our own selves.
Unfortunately, life not only sets its own rules; it
allows us to interpret those rules; all too often the
interpreter will believe that he must compromise,
that life's rules demand that he act with expedience.

Afterwards he will say to himself, or anyone else
who may be interested, "I had to do it; there just
wasn't any other way." Most of polite society will
agree with him; certainly none will be impolite
enough to contradict him. But there was, and is,
another way, as is attested to by the existence of
such paragons as Sallie Nichols is attempting to
describe. Strangely enough, many of them do very
nicely, at least when judged by a yardstick of
which they would approve.

Our concern here is not with the face of man in
the streets of everyday, but with the face of man

in the pages of books—and not just any face: the face of the hero. Unfortunately, with the exception of myths and fairy tales, literary heroes do not, for the most part, individuate. Some, like David Copperfield, grow up and attain relative maturity; others, like John Galsworthy's Soames Forsyte, grow old and relatively mellow. Most remain unchanging, but, if we may be allowed the cliché, there is always an exception to every rule. "Uncle Pierre! Oh! what a wonderful person he is!" (33, p. 1399) These words are spoken—or thought—near the end of Tolstoy's *War and Peace*; Uncle Pierre is, of course, Pierre Bezuhov.

At first glance it might seem strange to jump backwards—from mid-twentieth century America, the Beat Generation and "Howl," to mid-nineteenth century Russia, Leo Tolstoy and *War and Peace*. But one of Tolstoy's primary concerns, particularly in the second half of his life, was with the damage that could be inflicted by a materialistic society on a "natural" man.

At this point we must be very clear that we are not simply speaking about social justice, a not-quite ubiquitous commodity in the mid-nineteenth century. Indeed, at that time even the concept of social justice was less than widespread; and where it existed at all could best be summed up in the words of that favorite hymn of the children of the "haves" of the world, "All Things Bright And Beautiful":

> The rich man in his castle, the poor man at his
> gate,

76

> He made them high or lowly, and ordered
>   their estate.

With this kind of concern for the children of the "have-nots," it is no wonder that much of the literary output of such contemporaries of Tolstoy's as Charles Dickens and Victor Hugo should be almost polemical in nature—a series of impassioned attempts to educate the people, to show them injustice, their injustice. And justice, in the fullest sense of the word, would be more a theme of Tolstoy's life than a mere literary concern.

But at this time we are primarily concerned, not with Tolstoy's feelings about justice, however strong they may have been, but with his perception of the danger to man—to man's potential, if you will—concomitant with his living in a society in which, as we have noted, compromise and expedience are all too often the order of the day. In this Tolstoy was, if not a prophet, at least many years ahead of his time. Had he been destined to live in the mid-twentieth century we could well imagine reading a selection of his essays and short stories entitled *The Air-Conditioned Nightmare.*

Furthermore, *War and Peace* could serve as a textbook for Jungian theory. In this instance Tolstoy was not merely ahead of his time; he was ahead of Jung, who would not be born until some twenty years after the completion of this magnum opus.

Before examining this opus—and the specific changes in the face of its hero, and that face's position within the frame of our overall theme—let

us examine the face, or rather the many faces, of
Leo Tolstoy; for his was a face, and a life, of extra-
ordinary duality. At times, indeed, it seemed as if
he was trying to position himself a full 180 degrees
from himself.

Count Leo Tolstoy was born in 1828. At sixteen
he entered university. At nineteen, disappointed
with formal instruction, he withdrew, not only to
manage his own education, but because this would
also make it easier for him to manage his country
estate. But the social whirl proved more attractive
than either higher education or estate-manage-
ment; and it was to society that he would devote
his energies for the next few years.

In the early 1850s, his disaffection with his own
life having come to a head, he joined the army.
At this time too, he started to take his writing
seriously.

When Tolstoy returned to his estate, he was
shocked at the almost total lack of education
available to the peasants. He started his own
schools, wrote his own textbooks, even published
a magazine in which he set forth his own theories
of education.

He was married in 1862 and would spend the
next several years managing his estates, fathering
thirteen children, and writing the masterpieces
destined to ensure his literary immortality—*War and
Peace* and *Anna Karenina*. Both are recognized as
great books; many consider the former, if not the

greatest, certainly one of the greatest masterpieces of all time.

It would seem that life was good and more than good. But the man who, years before, had run to the army to escape the lures of society was once again becoming disaffected with life. Like others before him and others who would follow, he was seeking not merely purpose, but worthwhile purpose—searching, in fact, for the meaning of life.

More and more he turned to the peasants, for whom he had always felt sympathy—and to God; but to a God so out of step with orthodox religion that in 1901 he was formally excommunicated. Even before this, he had stopped smoking and drinking and become a vegetarian. He strove, in so far as it was possible for a landed aristocrat with a large income, to lead the self-sufficient life of a simple peasant.

A new kind of fame spread. He attracted followers—converts ready to embrace the Tolstoyean ideal of freeing oneself of the tyranny of possessions and adopting an ascetic life style. His wife was not numbered among them. Although he refused to publish any of his new writings, she obtained the copyright to everything written before 1880. Her husband might choose asceticism—her family would enjoy secure comfort.

In old age Tolstoy came to feel that the ease of life as head of a wealthy family mocked his professed ideals. Finally, accompanied by his doctor and one of his daughters, he attempted to steal away—to escape to the life of a recluse, to live according to his conception of goodness, to live as his wife would not allow him to live. He never found his refuge—he died of pneumonia in a country railway station.

So much for the author, the landed aristocrat who dreamed of becoming a peasant, the sensualist turned puritan. Is it any wonder that when writing his greatest work he needed two main characters in order to portray himself?

> In the way Tolstoy has of walking through all his books, in *War And Peace* he may be identified with the two heroes, Pierre and Prince Andrei, in their passionate, unremitting strivings towards "the infinite, the eternal and the absolute" (33, Introduction).

Before examining the "unremitting strivings" of Pierre and Prince Andrei, we should have some idea of the framework in which they took place. It would be unfair to say that ostensibly *War And Peace*, which covers the years 1805-1814, is about the lives, in peace, of a handful of Russian families, and the effect of war on those families. Rather, the book sets out to be about family and individual life in war and in peace, and it succeeds quite brilliantly. In this very, very long book, there are very, very many characters. Fortunately we are only concerned with the three main ones—the "stars" if you will: Natasha Rostov, Pierre Bezuhov, Prince Andrei Bolkonsky.

Prince Andrei is a polished aristocrat, self-assured in society, intellectually assured in his mind. Pierre, on the other hand, is a legitimatized bastard; he is not very good in society, and in his own mind far from assured. In the course of the book, Pierre will be maneuvered into a disastrous marriage, Prince Andrei and Natasha will become engaged, but the engagement will be broken, Prince Andrei will die a hero's death, nursed all the while by Natasha, with whom he has become reconciled; at the end of the book Pierre will marry Natasha. And now, "Everything about Pierre will belong to him. Nothing about him will be superimposed. Everything that he says or does will arise from his deepest center."

Not only has Pierre Bezuhov individuated, he has done so a good half-century and more before Carl Gustav Jung, in adopting the word for his own use, mapped out the steps to be taken en route to individuation. And Yet Pierre has followed those steps. Furthermore, not many years after the appearance of Tolstoy's great "novel of individuation" Dostoevsky would publish what many still regard as the greatest psychological novel ever written, *The Brothers Karamazov*. This at a time when Freud and Jung were still waiting in the wings—when psychology, as we understand it, had not yet been born.

If twentieth-century psychology was unknown, the concept of wholeness, of man becoming more, of man realizing the fullness of his potential, was as old as history—even older than Western history, as old, in India, as the Vedas. Jung would have been the first to acknowledge this. Even a casual reader of his *Collected Works* must be struck by the fact that, while the writer was interested in and capable of discoursing on virtually everything under the sun, his overriding interest—nay, passion—was with wholeness, with man realizing his potential. A great many of Jung's writings concern alchemy and the attempts of its practitioners to transmute the base metal, the lead of animal man, into the gold that is man's potential.

Furthermore, Jung's works are replete with Sanskrit words and concepts. But while acknowledging that the wisdom of the East has long been concerned with man's upward striving, Jung is very wary of the Eastern path. Indeed he almost demands that the West accept the Western way— the way of gnosticism and alchemy, of the Kabbalah and esoteric Christianity. At times he would even "explain" Eastern concepts to Eastern gurus and then complain that they couldn't understand, or wouldn't accept, his explanation of their truth. At one time he went so far as to reinterpret Kundalini Yoga:

> However with today's much better knowledge of Eastern thought, it is doubtful that Jung's "rope trick" of standing Kundalini Yoga on its head and then lopping off the two last chakras as "superfluous speculations with no practical value" would be accepted. (7, p. 123)

In making the above statement, Harold Coward is, of course, one hundred percent correct. In 1932

when Jung delivered his lecture on Kundalini, the
majority of his viewers would have had the haziest
conception of the meaning of the word. We can
only speculate as to whether Jung was presenting
a genuinely held belief, or whether he had "manu-
factured" an interpretation which would, in Harold
Coward's words, "cure the intellectual indiges-
tion" of his 1932 students; and also, and perhaps
more importantly, protect them from an ill-pre-
pared investigation of a discipline that today we
know to be potentially dangerous.

Whatever the truth may be, none of this should
be read as a criticism of Jung. He was not only
aware but appreciative of Eastern concepts; he
made frequent use of Sanskrit terms. Furthermore,
his sincerity is obvious in every line that he ever
wrote—he was convinced that when it came to
Self-realization, West could travel only so far with
East; and he honestly believed that danger, if not
disaster, awaited the Westerner who tried to tread
the Eastern path.

Jung's relationship with Eastern thought has
been introduced to reinforce the main theme of
this book: the face of the hero, or of heroes sprung
from the archetype represented by Odysseus, is
changing—is, in fact becoming more "Eastern."
That this is true is confirmed by seven words in
the first line of the above quote, "today's much
better knowledge of Eastern thought." Were an
interested researcher to accost the average teenager
on the average city street, the latter may never
have heard of individuation, but he could almost
certainly come up with at least one Eastern con-

cept. That concept might only be Kung Fu, but even then there would be a good chance of the teenager in question knowing that there was more to Kung Fu than merely battering through boards with his head.

We are moving ahead of ourselves, both in real time and in terms of this chapter. Furthermore, *War And Peace* is an example, not of Eastern Self-realization but of Jungian individuation. But before briefly examining the book in those terms we must outline the symbolic roles to be played by our three principals.

In the introduction to her translation of *War And Peace*, Rosemary Edwards points out that Prince Andrei and Pierre Bezuhov represent opposing sides of Tolstoy's own nature: in a sense they are one character. With this in mind, it is easy to expand this concept into, as it were, Jungian territory: Prince Andrei is at once himself, and Pierre's shadow;[1] and Pierre is at once himself, and Prince Andrei's shadow. (A similar situation exists in Marie-Louise von Franz's interpretation of the fairy tale "Faithful Johannes," outlined in Chapter 10 of this book.)

As for Natasha Rostov—if one excepts such mythic figures as Rider Haggard's "She," there is perhaps no better example of anima figure in all of literature. How inevitable that Prince Andrei

---

[1] In *Shadow and Evil in Fairytales* Marie-Louise von Franz discusses this aspect of the shadow, i.e. joint protagonists who are each other's shadow.

should love her—and how logical that Pierre
should love her too; for are they not protagonist
and shadow, shadow and protagonist?

War And Peace is not rich merely in archetypal
figures; it is rich too in the kind of symbols that
would forever fascinate Jung. There is even a tree
that plays a not insignificant role:

> It was an enormous tree, double a man's span,
> with ancient scars where branches had long
> ago been lopped off and bark stripped away.
> With huge ungainly limbs sprawling unsym-
> metrically, with gnarled hands and fingers, it
> stood, an aged monster, angry and scornful,
> among the smiling birch-trees. This Oak alone
> refused to yield to the season's spell, spurning
> both spring and sunshine. (33, p. 492)
>
> . . .
>
> "Yes, that old oak with which I saw eye to
> eye was here in this forest," thought Prince
> Andrei. "But whereabouts?" he wondered
> again, looking at the left side of the road and,
> without recognizing it, admiring the very oak
> he sought. The old oak, quite transfigured,
> spread out a canopy of dark, sappy green, and
> seemed to swoon and sway in the rays of the
> evening sun. There was nothing to be seen
> now of knotted fingers and scars, of old doubts
> and sorrows. Through the rough, century-old
> bark, even where there were no twigs, leaves
> had sprouted, so juicy, so young that it was
> hard to believe that aged veteran had borne
> them.
> "Yes, it is the same oak," thought Prince
> Andrei, and all at once he was seized by an ir-
> rational, spring-like feeling of joy and renewal.
> (33, p. 496)

85

For Prince Andrei the message of the old oak is, of course, personal: a specific message from a specific tree to a specific man. But for mankind the symbolic tree has manifold meaning, as Jung so clearly saw:

> Taken on average, the commonest associations to its meaning are growth, life, unfolding of form in a physical and spiritual sense, development, growth from below upwards and from above downwards. (17, p. 272)

> · · ·

> Similarly, the "Consilium Coniugii," commenting on Senior, says: "Thus the stone is perfected of and in itself. For it is the tree whose branches, leaves, flowers, and fruits come from it and through it and for it, and it is itself whole (tota vel totum) and nothing else." Hence the tree is identical with the stone and, like it, a symbol of wholeness. (17, p. 319)

> · · ·

> In so far as the tree symbolizes the opus and the transformation process "tam ethice quam physice" (both morally and physically), it also signifies the life process in general. Its identity with Mercurius, the *spiritus vegetativus*, confirms this view. Since the opus is a life, death, and rebirth mystery, the tree as well acquires this significance and in addition the quality of wisdom. (17, p. 339)

Who among us could conceive of a more perfect symbol of wholeness than the tree? As the above quotes point out, each tree is perfect in itself; as a seed, it grows from above downwards, stretching its roots into Grandmother Earth, whose wisdom will not only sustain it, but teach it to stretch its arms to Grandfather Sky—to the wisdom of the

Spirit. If individuation is an "opus" of transfor-
mation, what better symbol than a tree, whose
growth and changing seasons of year and of century reflect birth, life, death, and rebirth?

As it happens, Prince Andrei will not live to
realize the wholeness so aptly symbolized by the
ancient oak, not, at any rate, as Prince Andrei. But
it could be argued that in some metaphysical manner he, or his spirit, will eventually do so as the
fully integrated shadow of Pierre Bezuhov; for it is
at approximately the time of Prince Andrei's dying
that Pierre is finally ready to integrate into his personal wholeness those "shadow" qualities necessary for his own successful individuation.

After coming to terms with the shadow, some
understanding must be reached with the anima.
That Pierre and Natasha become man and wife is
unlikely to surprise even the most obtuse of
readers. This union was inevitable from the first
moment they saw one another; and when the time
is right, protagonist and anima must unite. Such a
union may not always betoken a new beginning,
though it often does; but it always signals the birth
of a larger and more meaningful wholeness—a continuation of odyssey on wider and more meaningful paths.

We know that for Pierre larger wholeness meant
successfully managing his estates, caring for his
peasants, looking after all who were dependent
upon him, and, above all, being a happily married
man. It is interesting in the light of Rosemary Edwards' observations to compare the Pierre Bezuhov

of the end of *War And Peace* with the Leo Tolstoy at the end of the writing of *War And Peace.* It is hard to tell where one ends and the other begins: the writer is the protagonist, the protagonist the writer.

Whereas Pierre may well continue to play the ideal squire, Tolstoy will go on to write *Anna Karenina,* in many ways a much darker work. By the end of this novel he will again be dissatisfied with his life. Though always the most compassionate of aristocrats and benefactor of the peasants, he will now wish for nothing more than to be himself a simple peasant, or, better still, an ascetic recluse.

It is interesting to compare this author/character duo with the author/character duo of Kazantzakis and Odysseus. Like Pierre, Tolstoy is forever seeking the meaningful, and having found it—or rather, believing that he has found it—he wants to stop right there. He wants to get off at the terminus marked ''Meaningful'' and go about the business of doing meaningful things. Kazantzakis, on the other hand, knows that there is no terminus whose name is ''Meaningful.'' On the contrary, ''Meaningful'' is the name of the path. ''Meaningful'' is finding that path which has a heart,[2] and following it forever upward. We have

---

[2] The importance of asking whether the path on which one finds oneself is ''a path with a heart'' is one of the teachings of Don Juan, and runs through the series of books written by Carlos Castenadas. See Bibliography.

only to recall how, at the end of Kazantzakis' great poem Odysseus:

> great mind leapt to the peak of its holy
>   freedom,
> fluttered with empty wings, then upright
>   through the air
> soared high and freed itself from its last cage
>   (19, p. 775).

8

A Fairy Tale Hero
("The Faithful Johannes," I)

*This is a tale beloved by the children of Japan, and
by the old folk—a tale of magical jewels and a visit to
the Sea King's palace.*
Grace James, "Green Willow"

*There was once upon a time a castle in the middle of
a thick wood where lived an old woman quite alone,
for she was an enchantress.*
Andrew Lang, The Green Fairy Book

It is only within the past few hundred years that
fairy tales have become the province of children.
Once upon a time they belonged to grown-ups.
Shamans and medicine-men and good witches, all
of whom were practicing psychology long before
Freud or Adler or Jung, carried with them—in their
minds—a library of such tales. They knew that
these were not merely just-so stories or fireside
yarns, but that they had evolved over long centuries and contained, in concentrated form, the wisdom of all those years.

Such tales—real fairy tales as opposed to the fiction of such as Hans Christian Andersen—are not
the property of a specific time, a specific place, or
a specific people: their time is every time, their
place everywhere, their people everyone.

Such a tale is "Faithful Johannes" (13). This is a
tale, as are all fairy tales, rich in implications for

the hero's inward journey. Its characters can be seen to depict aspects of his psyche, and his adventures are steps along his path toward individuation. Over the years, the story of "Faithful Johannes" has been approached from many angles. We shall examine two: the Christian-mystic interpretation of General Ethan Allen Hitchcock, and the Jungian interpretation of Marie-Louise van Franz. Then we shall offer a third: employing esoteric concepts and such terminology as may be necessary, we shall interpret "Faithful Johannes" in terms of Self-realization. First, it is necessary to tell the story in brief.

Before dying, an old king calls to his bedside his trusted servant, Faithful Johannes. "Look after my son," he says. "Serve him faithfully. Show him all the rooms of this palace, except the room wherein is hidden the portrait of the Princess of the Golden Roof. If he sees that portrait he will instantly fall in love; then he will faint; and then who knows what may happen?"

After the death of the old king, Faithful Johannes is unable to dissuade the new king from entering the forbidden room. He therefore takes the key from the great bunch of keys which hangs from his belt and opens the door. The young king sees the portrait of the Princess of the Golden Roof. He instantly falls in love, and then faints. As soon as he recovers consciousness, he begs Faithful Johannes to help him win the hand of the princess.

The Princess loves gold; accordingly Faithful Johannes has a ship loaded with beautiful golden

91

articles, and he and the young king, who is now disguised as a merchant, set sail.

When they arrive at their destination, the king stays on the ship and Faithful Johannes, having first filled his apron with golden trinkets, goes in search of the princess. When he shows her the trinkets, she is so delighted she agrees to return to the ship with Faithful Johannes in order to view all the other golden objects.

Enchanted by these, the princess does not at first notice that the ship has set sail. When she finally realizes what has happened, the king is quick to allay her fears. ''I am not a merchant, I am a king as well born as yourself. When I saw your portrait, I fainted with love.''

The Princess of the Golden Roof agrees to marry the king. All would seem to be well; but when Faithful Johannes is on deck he overhears the conversation of three ravens.

The first says that on landing the king will see a beautiful chestnut horse and want to ride it, but if he does he will never see the princess again. The only way he can be saved is for someone else to jump on the horse first. There will be a pistol in its holster on the saddle, and this person must shoot the horse.

The second raven says that if he is saved, he will see bridal apparel that appears to be made of silver and gold, but in reality is woven of sulfur and pitch. If the king puts it on, he will be burned to the marrow. The only hope is for someone wearing gloves to throw the deceptive garment into the fire.

The third raven says there would still be danger, for at the wedding ball the princess will turn pale and fall down as though dead, and unless someone sucks three drops of blood from her right breast, she will die. All three ravens warn that if anyone tells the king of these dangers, that person will be turned to stone from his toes to his heart.

As the ravens pass out of earshot, Faithful Johannes resolves that, even if it costs him his own life, he will save his master.

As the royal party come ashore, the predictions of the ravens begin to come true. The king starts to mount a magnificent chestnut horse he finds on the shore, but Faithful Johannes springs into the saddle, draws the pistol, and shoots the horse.

This angers the king's other servants, all of whom have long been jealous of Faithful Johannes; but the king himself decides to forgive and forget.

When they reach the palace, the king sees what appears to be a bridal garment of gold and silver; however before he can touch it Faithful Johannes, wearing gloves, takes it to the fire and burns it. The king is angered by this incident, and the other servants protest, but the king decides once again to forgive and forget.

However, when the prophecy of the third raven comes true, the sight of his servant sucking three drops of blood from his bride's right breast is too much for the king: he orders that Faithful Johannes be put to death.

Before he is led to the gallows, Faithful Johannes demands the right to speak, a right accorded to all condemned men. The king on hearing the whole story immediately forgives Faithful Johannes. But the fourth prophecy of the ravens has already come true: Faithful Johannes has been turned to stone.

The contrite king has the stone statue placed in his bedroom. Every time he looks at it, he weeps and wishes that there were some way he could bring his faithful servant back to life.

Time passes. The queen gives birth to twin sons, who are a delight to their parents. One day when the queen has gone alone to church, the king wishes out loud that he could bring Faithful Johannes back to life. This time the statue speaks to him and says that this can be done, but the king must sacrifice that which he holds most dear. He must cut off his children's heads and daub the statue with their blood. The horrified king remembers Johannes' sacrifice. He draws his sword, beheads the twins, and daubs the statue with blood.

On returning to life, Johannes picks up the children's heads, puts them back in place and daubs the wounds with blood. The children immediately start playing happily.

When he hears his wife returning, the overjoyed king hides Faithful Johannes and the twins in a big cupboard. The queen tells him that while in church she was saddened by thoughts of their dear Faithful Johannes. The king tells her that their servant can be brought back to life, but only by the sacrifice of their children. The queen turns pale with horror, but she agrees that Faithful Johannes deserves even this sacrifice.

The cupboard door is thrown open. Faithful Johannes and the twins emerge.

They all live happily ever after.

9

A Christian John
("The Faithful Johannes," II)

*It is certain...and this should be well considered,
that the best of ancient learning was couched in proverbs and parables.*

. . .

*It may just be remarked here, that while some of
the Fairy and other tales, recently brought to light,
have a heathen origin, probably in part Druidical,
and some have what is called a profane or unreligious
source, there are others again, which are like those of
the "Gesta Romanorum," entirely Christian in their
character, for which we are undoubtedly indebted to
the monks of the middle ages, who were at one time
in possession of most of the libraries and nearly all
the learning of the Christian world.*

Gen. Ethan Allen Hitchcock

These words were first published in 1865 in *The Red Book of Appin: A Story of the Middle Ages with Other Hermetic Stories and Allegorical Tales*, in an age when muscular Christianity was alive and well and living wherever Anglo-Saxons congregated—and in 1866 Anglo-Saxons congregated in a great many places. Surely there could have been few whose Christianity was as muscular as that of the book's author, General Ethan Allen Hitchcock, who held that "our book of life...belongs to another, to whom we must deliver it when summoned by Him." Yet, as Manly Palmer Hall has pointed out,

The Faithful Johannes

General Hitchcock was among the first Western
thinkers to explore the abstract realm of archetypal
symbolism, and to realize that fairy tales and oriental mandalas had secret and valuable meanings.
Obviously, he was not concerned with either individuation or Self-realization per se—the first edition
of *The Red Book of Appin* appeared in 1865, ten
years before the birth of Carl Gustav Jung. But he
was concerned with the journey and questing spirit
of man.

General Hitchcock's enthusiasm was greatest
when exploring a Christian path, but he was nevertheless aware of others:

> There cannot be a shadow of a doubt that the
> story of the voyage of Sinbad was originally
> conceived and written for the purpose of illus-
> trating, figuratively and symbolically, the pas-
> sage of man from a state of bondage in
> ignorance to a condition of freedom in light
> and knowledge, as conceived under the in-
> fluence of Eastern religions or persuasions.
> (15, p. 262)

Still, his Christian bias is very strong. The general's interpretation of "Faithful Johannes" is
based on the translation contained in *Grimm's
Popular Tales*, which was published in 1862. In this
version Faithful Johannes is anglicized; and in the
general's interpretation Faithful John is none other
than John the Evangelist, or rather the personification of the Gospel according to St. John:

> The faithful John, here referred to, is John the
> Evangelist, the loved disciple of the Lord, who

> now lives in the faithful history of his Master;
> and the declaration, "Let faithful John come to
> me," imports that the aged man, [the dying
> king] feeling the infirmities of declining years,
> or that want of spiritual rest so common to
> those who are called men of the world, has
> turned his attention to the Gospel, or to the
> writings of John in particular, and being con-
> vinced of the fidelity or faithfulness of John, he
> determines to yield himself to the influence of
> the teachings of the Gospel, and describes this
> purpose under the figure of calling faithful
> John to his bedside. (15, p. 148)

The general prefaces his interpretation with three
possibilities for the meaning of the old king and
the son: that the king is simply an aged man and
his son the old man's soul; that the son signifies
Israel or the soul of the human race; or that the
old king represents the letter of the law about to
give place to his spirit in the form of his son.

From this we can see that the general was capable of varied interpretations at different levels.
However, he chooses the first one:

> But we shall assume the first of the above
> suppositions—that the old King represents a
> man, whose "care" for his Son signifies his
> *concern* for his soul—the interpretation in the
> main answering to all three of the suppositions
> (15, p. 143).

In the interpretation we learn that the injunction
of the old king to Faithful John expresses the former's faith in the power of the gospel to disclose

to a faithful soul its own spiritual wonders, and that we are to follow the path of that soul under the guidance of the gospel:

> up stairs and down stairs (through heaven and earth)...all the splendid chambers;—to wit, the new Jerusalem as described in Revelation; for the new Jerusalem is the "paternal mansion" of the soul,—when understood in the spirit, which "giveth life" (15, p. 151).

We are told that the beauty of the portrait of the Princess of the Golden Roof is a mystical allusion to the beauty of the twentieth chapter of John's gospel; that the key to the door of the room in which that portrait is contained is Christ, and that the bunch of keys from which *the* key is selected is the books of the Bible.

It is, of course, not easy to attain that eternal life which is symbolized by the "Princess of the Golden Roof":

> Everything that she has around her is of gold; that is, within the sphere of the King's daughter, nothing is seen or known but virgin truth, figured by gold. The seeker is told, in one word, to fill his soul with truth; and this law is absolute. Everything false must be expelled from the heart that would know the truth or come in its presence. (15, p. 154)

After adopting suitable disguises (which would seem a strange way of obeying the absolute law of expelling all that is not true from the heart), Faithful John and the young king set off across the wide seas of the world.

In a mystical sense the king and John are one and the same, and when, after reaching their destination, the King is told to remain on the ship, this signifies that in the search for truth man must not go out of himself or out of his true nature.

In due course Faithful John is conducted to the Princess; and when she sees his treasures she asks to be taken to the ship.

> In this declaration, "take me to the ship," we must recognize a soul, which, having seen some of the beauties of spiritual life...determines to pass wholly to a higher life, in order the more completely to realize its spiritual treasures (15, p. 160).

Even a cursory reading of the above quotes will demonstrate with what thoroughness the General approaches his self-appointed task. Every aspect of every character is studied from every angle. Every glance is dissected. Every material object is turned upside down—examined inside and out.

How strange, then, that in this interpretation of "Faithful Johannes," the three ravens, recast as three crows in the "Faithful John" translation, are never even mentioned—the general glides smoothly past them.

He excuses himself from any mention of black birds, and proceeds to interpret the end of the story with exactly the same degree of thoroughness that he lavished on the beginning, thus reinforcing our curiosity as to the omission of the birds.

We have only to read a few lines of *The Red Book of Appin* to realize that, whether we agree or disagree with the interpretation offered, its author is an expert in his chosen field. As an expert, therefore, he must have realized—indeed demonstrates his realization in every line that he writes— that whenever, in a fairy tale, creatures are mentioned by name, those creatures have a specific allegorical or symbolical meaning; the same is true of numbers. Why three ravens? Surely one talking bird would have sufficed—a chatty seagull for instance. And why birds in the first place—why not a friendly seal, or a flying fish? And overriding all other whys—why avoid any mention of these three important characters?

The number three is easily understood. It is an odd number, therefore it is masculine. Indeed in some schools of numerology three is regarded as the first masculine number, one being accepted more as an indication of unity—the oneness from which all other numbers emanate. We may therefore safely accept that, at some stage in the evolution of "Faithful Johannes," the masculine quality of the messengers—or perhaps of the message itself—was deemed important. (Other, more esoteric meanings of the number three are discussed supra, specifically in connection with Nikos Kazantzakis.)

However, ravens—or for that matter crows— provide us with a more complex symbol. In *The*

101

A Christian John

Phenomenology of The Spirit in Fairytales Jung says, in connection with the raven:

> ...but his soul is in the power of an evil spirit, a sinister father-imago of subterrene nature in the guise of a raven, the celebrated theriomorphic figure of the devil (17, p. 240).

In *Shadow and Evil in Fairytales* Marie-Louise von Franz tells us:

> In the Middle Ages, as in many other mythological fields, this archetypal symbol of the raven has been cut in two, into a light and dark aspect. It is both a symbol of the devil and of a dark mystical spiritual connectedness with God. In Greek mythology the raven belongs, amazingly enough, to the sun God Apollo and again represents his winter side, his dark Boreal side.
>
> The raven is thus a messenger of the more unknown, the darker, less shining and more invisible side of the great God. Melancholy, deep thoughts, and evil thoughts are very close to each other; the effect of loneliness is both a pre-condition for possession by evil and, for exceptional people who know how to behave in it, a pre-condition for reaching the inner center. The raven might lead either to possession by evil or into essential inner realizations which are always the dark side of the sun God, i.e., thoughts not dominant in collective consciousness at the moment, which the collective would look upon as evil.''
> (35, p. 212)

It is not difficult to understand why General Hitchcock elected not to interpret the three ravens:

in his reading of "Faithful John" everything be-
speaks of goodness and light, of the gospel guid-
ing the soul of man on the path of righteousness.
There is simply no room at his inn for ravens,
"theriomorphic figures of the devil," or any other
black-winged messengers of a "darker, more invisible, less shining face of the great God."

The great god in question is, of course, Apollo.
We shall shortly see that, not only was the general
prepared to look at the face of Islam, but he was
prepared to interpret that face with relative impar-
tiality. But how would he have felt about the face
of pagan Zeus—or an age of mystery religions
whose adherents accepted that not all faces of God
were brightly shining—that deity too had its
shadow side?

Whatever the general may have felt, his difficulties would have been compounded by the fact
that though these birds may have come from symbolic darkness their message was not unfriendly.
How could he accept that "messengers from the
dark side" could actually be helpful? Though we
shall return to these birds, we may well understand why General Hitchcock eschews both ravens
and their warning and proceeds directly to a discussion of the three dangers which yet await the
young king and his bride-to-be.

The fox-colored horse of the general's translation
represents spiritual pride; it carries with it the
weapon by which it may be put to death, "for
every man must be, for himself, the executioner of
his own pride."

The second danger concerns the delusion
that one can obtain righteousness from any
outer source, the delusive imagination that the
soul is "itself excused from being instrumental
in clothing itself with its proper 'wedding gar-
ments,' in which to appear at the marriage of
the Son" (15, p. 163).

The third danger is of feeling one can live in
the world without a true spiritual foundation,
not merely "the letter of the law":

The fallacy of this is represented by the
attempt of the bride to engage in the dance,
the symbol of action in life, in which attempt
she suddenly finds her power fails her, and,
turning pale, she falls down as if dead.

But here also the Gospel, in the person of
faithful John, is at hand, and applies the proper remedy by casting away three drops of
blood from the right breast of the bride; a mysterious symbol indicating a casting away of the
three principles by which the *one* is restored to
life and action. (15, p. 163)

From the above quotes it will be seen that, having detoured around those pesky ravens, the general is resolved to be as thorough as he was before
their entrance; furthermore, provided that it has no
awkward attachments, he is prepared to ascribe
symbolic meaning to the number three; and that
his hero is not so crass as to actually *suck* the three
drops of blood from the bride's right breast.

Finally the sacrifice required of the young king in
order to restore faithful John to life is likened to
that required of the patriarch, Abraham; and we
are told that the two sons, restored to life by the
providence of God, represent reason and affection.

The Faithful Johannes

This book is concerned with the inner and outer journeys of man. As one of the earliest mappers of certain aspects of those journeys, General Hitchcock belongs in these pages. The following passage not only captures the flavor of General Hitchcock's writing, it also reveals the working of his mind in his interpretations of symbology:

> We must consider that in this story of Faithful John, visible children according to the flesh are only used figuratively, or as symbolical of spiritual children—children of the soul. This whole story has reference to the spiritual nature of man, which develops itself in two chief directions; one, manifesting the reason, or the truly active side of life; the other, exhibiting the passional, or passive side of life. These two modes of life are often apparently diverse in phenomenal nature, but they are essentially one in the true life; and the great object of instruction is to bring about in the individual a perfect harmony between the reason and the affections, or an approximation of it, as far as the limited nature of man will allow. This is not accomplished by the action of either by itself, but may be affected through the intervention of a perfectly simple but mysterious third principle, figured in Exodus as an Angel, in whom, as we read, God's word resides.
>
> We can bestow no higher praise upon any man than by saying that his affections act in harmony with reason; not merely with *his* reason, but with reason itself. (15, p. 166)

One may agree or disagree with General Hitchcock's interpretation. At times, indeed, it is difficult not to feel that he is forcing incidents in the story to conform to his Christian vision. Then again much the same thing will be found in examining the Jungian approach of Marie-Louise von Franz, to be discussed next; and whatever one may think of *The Red Book of Appin*, it is impossible not to be fascinated by its contents, and to admire the dedication and scholarly approach of its author.

10

The Jungian Self
("The Faithful Johannes," III)

The concept of individuation plays a large role in our psychology. In general, it is the process by which individual beings are formed and differentiated; in particular it is the development of the psychological individual *as a being distinct from the general, collective psychology. Individuation, therefore, is a process of* differentiation *having for its goal the development of the individual personality.*

C.G. Jung

Marie-Louise von Franz has this much in common with Ethan Allen Hitchcock: her eponymous hero is also named John rather than Johannes. From here on, however, the psychologist and the general tread very different paths; for although the interpretation contained in *The Red Book of Appin* describes a mystic-Christian process not unrelated to individuation, and while, by the tale's conclusion, the young king has indeed individuated, individuation per se is not, in this instance, the focus of von Franz's interest. The chapter where she discusses this fairy tale is headed "The Surrender of Ego" and the book containing that chapter is entitled *Shadow and Evil in Fairytales.* This being the interpretive route chosen by Dr. von Franz, we should, before proceeding, define these terms. The shadow is the unconscious darker side of the personality, but it is not all evil. Joseph L. Henderson makes this clear:

> Dr. Jung has pointed out that the shadow cast by the conscious mind of the individual contains the hidden, repressed, and unfavorable (or nefarious) aspects of the personality. But this darkness is not just the simple converse of the conscious ego. Just as the ego contains unfavorable and destructive attitudes, so the shadow has good qualities—normal instincts and creative impulses. Ego and shadow, indeed, although separate, are inextricably linked together in much the same way that thought and feeling are related to each other. (18, p. 118)

Jung himself gives the following definition of ego and self:

> By ego I understand a complex of ideas which constitutes the centre of my field of consciousness, and appears to possess a high degree of continuity and identity. I distinguish between the ego and the *self*, since the ego is only the subject of my consciousness, while the self is the subject of my total psyche, which also includes the unconscious. (17, p. 425)

So, according to this definition (Jung has given others), the self is the total psyche, while the ego is the conscious part with which we usually identify. The shadow is unconsciousness, the repressed aspects of the ego.

Oriental Self-realization and Jungian individuation are not identical, but they are compatible. The

realization of the Self mentioned in the above definition is the to-be-desired end of the path of individuation—a path which the young king could not
walk without Faithful John, nor indeed Faithful
John without the young king. In von Franz's interpretation, "John and the prince are each other's
shadows."

However, Faithful John is more than merely
hero, and hero's shadow. Von Franz explains that
"the name 'John'...comes from the medieval
Jewish legend of Rabbi Johannan, who helped
King Solomon," so that "John, the maker of the
new king, is a kind of priest-medicine man personality" (35, p. 68). She goes on to equate him with
a special creative function in the unconscious that
can reconcile opposites:

> Faithful John is a kind of personification of that
> part of the unconscious which has a tendency
> to build up a new conscious position; we
> might call him the creative spirit in the uncon-
> scious...We could call him a personification of
> what Jung calls the transcendent function, that
> which can unite the opposite positions
> (35, p. 73).

Von Franz likens Faithful John to Khidr, and to
Mercurius,[1] thereby linking Islam and alchemy.
This is typical of her interpretation; it is a plexus of
folk-lore and religion, wisdom and superstition. It

---

[1]Khidr was an Islamic prophet who lived at the time of Moses.
The figure of Mercurius is discussed at length by Jung, in particular in the volumes of his *Collected Works* devoted to Alchemy (Volumes 12, 13 and 14). This figure (Mercurius) is also
extensively discussed in Parts 1 and 2 of Vol. 9.

is difficult within the limitations of a synopsis to capture its richness. With this caveat, and bearing in mind the many faces of Faithful John, let us proceed.

The old king, representative of the, until now, dominant force of collective consciousness, is dying. This is an all-masculine world. The only hint of a female is an anima figure, a portrait hidden behind the locked doors of a forbidden room. The beginning of our fairy tale, therefore, accurately mirrors late Christianity, particularly Protestantism, which, like exoteric Judaism, contains no feminine element. (In Catholicism, thanks to the Virgin Mary, the situation is not quite so extreme.)

This position is reflected in General Hitchcock's interpretation. Von Franz laments the repression of the earth mother figure who appears in all pagan cults, the shadow aspect of the feminine principle. The mother image of the Virgin Mary represents only that which is beautiful and pure. The fairy tale reflects for von Franz our civilization: the ruling principle (the old king) is losing strength, and even the image of a woman (a necessary element of wholeness) is hidden away.

The young king sees in the castle only the portrait of the Princess of the Golden Roof. The real woman is beyond the sea—far, far away from the shores of consciousness. To cross that sea and lure the princess aboard ship is one thing; to bring her safely to the mainland of everyday reality quite

110

another, for this implies integrating all that she symbolizes.

Unlike General Hitchcock, von Franz does not detour around the three ravens; indeed she specifically states that she cannot "skip" them. These birds of Apollo were used for divination; they have connections with telepathy and parapsychology—with the unconscious mind. And like the unconscious they talk to one another rather than to the conscious mind. Not everyone can hear the voice of the unconscious. Fortunately for the young king, Faithful John can. Von Franz sees the princess as in danger because she is bewitched so that her body has become poisonous. The evil magic must be exorcised before the young king can safely marry her. This theme is archetypal, a common element in oriental legends and in northern European countries, where often the princess had an affair with a pagan demon who lives in the woods. Von Franz gives this bewitchment a psychological interpretation: "Psychologically, you can say that she is contaminated with unconscious impulses which want to become conscious and, because they are not, they get at the man's emotional side and influence his moods" (35, p. 68). The feminine needs to be brought to consciousness.

Thus far our anima has been merely "The Princess of the Golden Roof." She has been high up. Now we encounter another side of her being, the red horse. The Princess is the Virgin Mary; she is also Mary Magdelene.

111

It is fortunate that it is Faithful John who will destroy the horse, for this horse must be approached in just the right manner. John represents the transcendent function, that which mediates between conscious and unconscious. All too often when the conscious mind, in this instance the young king, attempts such a task, the result is that the passions break free, and, wilder than ever, roam at will across the land. Or, even more dangerously, not across the land but into a state of unreality,

> up into the air—a kind of Pegasus which takes one away from the earth, reality. Physical passion, if really carried by the anima, does not lead to reality because the anima is an image and because the divine quality of the anima leads to possession and unreality. (35, p. 87)

Here we are obviously dealing with a Jungian and not a Freudian interpretation. Freud believed that such "red horses" must either be controlled or sublimated by the conscious mind. Jung, on the other hand, believed that such creatures of the unconscious contain within themselves the possibility of their own sacrifice. It is fitting, therefore, and no doubt satisfying to Jungians, that the pistol carried by the horse is intended, and will be used, for its own destruction.

Like General Hitchcock before her, Marie-Louise von Franz has, until this moment, analyzed every aspect of this story; now, like the general at an earlier point in the same story, she almost completely bypasses the surely not insignificant bridal garment and poisoned right breast. This can hardly be intentional; there are, after all, any number of symbolic readings which would support her view. Perhaps the bridal shirt is simply too obvious to merit attention; she has dealt specifically with the number three, and by implication, with the "sucking of contamination" from the anima figure. Or perhaps we should bear in mind that *Shadow and Evil in Fairytales* was put together from a series of lectures delivered at the Jung Institute in Zurich—a circumstance which makes this omission easy to understand. Or perhaps she was merely anxious to get to the petrification of John, for this obviously intrigues her:

> Why must Faithful John be petrified? One feels that a curse lies at the bottom of it. (37, p. 89)

In exploring this situation, von Franz looks first at our Christian civilization, then at Sigmund Freud, and then at the fact that the young king and queen place the petrified statue in their bedroom; but although sex is often an important—at times indeed the most important—aspect of the problem here represented, we should not lose sight of other aspects:

> The king and queen cannot meet completely, then, because between them a petrified figure always watches reproachfully and gives them such feelings of guilt that they cannot enjoy their life together.
> The petrification of Faithful John can also be seen wherever the dominating principle of consciousness does not recognize the ever-chang-

113

> ing aspect of the unconscious, for this failure
> of vision has a petrifying effect on the uncon-
> scious. (35, p. 90)

The children that the king must sacrifice to save
Faithful John represent his own future possibility,
even as did Isaac to Abraham. What is required
then is the greatest possible sacrifice; for surely,
like Abraham, the king would rather kill himself
than his children.

At this point Faithful John—Khidr, Mercurius,
shadow-hero and hero-shadow—reveals who he
really is: an image of God. For to whom other
than God himself would one make so great a sacrifice? If every character in this story—whether human, animal, or bird, even the castle—is an aspect
of the king, does he, and by extension, do we,
contain within an aspect of God?

The old king, or that which was the king, is
dying. He is ready to become more than he was—
to grow, to individuate, to make way for the rule
of the potentially greater self represented by the
young king. With the help of Faithful John, who
rescues many aspects of himself, this individuation
is almost achieved. But somehow our hero has lost
contact with his unconscious, and with it perhaps
that portion of the godhead which lives in him. To
be whole—to be the greater self he has sought to
be, to achieve his individuation—he must regain
contact with all that Faithful John now symbolizes.
A great sacrifice is needed, and what greater
sacrifice can there be than his own children, his

own potential for growth and for further individuation—even as he as son once filled this role for the old king?

Once the sacrifice was made, the children are restored to life, and they all live happily ever after—or at least until the children, like the young prince at our story's beginning, are ready to assume *their* estate, to move on to yet more potential and wholeness.

Marie-Louise von Franz's interpretation is full of fascinating side-roads and is much richer than can be indicated here. Furthermore, one should bear in mind that she is not discussing individuation per se, but shadow and evil. Nevertheless, whereas our tale began with three men, one of whom was dying, and contained but the palest hint of a female figure, we have, at the end a quaternity—a symbol of wholeness comprising father, mother, Faithful John, and two children who can be counted as a unit since they both represent the future potential of the composite protagonist. For the time being at least, our hero has achieved wholeness—has, therefore, successfully individuated.

11

An Esoteric Composite
("The Faithful Johannes," IV)

Oh, East is East, and West is West, and never the
twain shall meet,
Till Earth and Sky stand presently at God's great
Judgement Seat;
But there is neither East nor West, Border, nor
Breed, nor Birth,
When two strong men stand face to face, though they
come from the ends of the earth!

Rudyard Kipling

"You worship a man," say the Lakota people, "who was born of a virgin, who was tortured and killed; yet who, on the third day, rose from the dead and walked among men in a body of flesh. This man, you tell us, is God. The one God. The only God. The God whose message is absolute truth.

"After we have listened we tell you of the coming of White Buffalo woman, and of her message.[1] Then you tell us that this is folklore—that our message is myth. Is what you tell us less impossible than what we tell you?"

At first glance it would seem that when it comes to religion, any number of strong men may stand

---

[1]For the story of White Buffalo Woman, and of the Buffalo who holds back the waters see *The Sacred Pipe: Black Elk's Account of the Seven Rites of the Oglala Sioux* (1).

116

face to face, and though they come not from the
ends of the earth but from neighboring villages,
alien concept will remain alien concept; after all,
both Christianity and the autochthonous religion of
the Lakota people must be accepted as Western.

But there is also the buffalo who stands at the
west—the buffalo who holds back the waters. In
the beginning this buffalo stood on four legs and
had a magnificent coat. But every year he loses a
hair from that coat; and at the end of every age, of
which there are four, he loses a leg. Today his coat
is almost gone, and he stands on one leg. Compare the buffalo of the Lakota with the four yugas
of Brahmanism, the four ages of the world, ages of
gold, silver, bronze, and iron. The Kali Yuga is the
fourth, "the *black* or iron age, our present
period...the last of the ages into which the evolutionary period of man is divided by a series of
such ages. (3, 170)

We stand at the midpoint of Kali Yuga, the black
age, and the waters of dissolution are being held
back by a feeble, one-legged buffalo. In terms of
religion, it is hard to go further east than Brahmanism, or further west than the indigenous peoples
of North America. And yet, how different are the
concepts of buffalo and yuga? In the introduction
to this book, it was pointed out, vis-a-vis the face
of the hero, that East and West are moving closer
together, that Luke Skywalker was as much the
product of Zen Buddhism as of U.S. technology.

As above, so below. If the Hermetic axiom is correct, then what is true for fiction should be true for

religion. And surely this is the case: the pendulum is swinging back. Once upon a time Western missionaries traveled east with word of the one God; now, in ever-increasing numbers Eastern missionaries come West with news, if not of the one God, then of the oneness of God. How often have we heard of the one mountain up which run many paths? The paths are different, but they all lead to the top of the same mountain, where all paths meet and become one. Perhaps we, and with us Faithful John, are closer to the mountain top than we realize.

We have seen that, as a parable, "Faithful Johannes" *works* both in terms of mystic Christianity and Jungian individuation. If this is also true when Eastern concepts are applied, then how far apart can our several paths be? Perhaps today it is only missionaries of the exoteric who still see narrow paths rather than a single broad road.

This should not be understood as meaning that individuation and Self-realization are identical. If this were true, then Jung would not have insisted that Westerners should follow a Western path, or attempted to "explain" aspects of their own path to Easterners.

The mandala plays a very important role in Jungian psychology. Perhaps it would not be inappropriate to allow the mandala, as symbol of individuation, to assist us in determining such differences as do exist between the two states. Picture a mandala. Combine this image with the thought that, in individuation, the personality is integrated around the center. The Jungian self is the center of the mandala.

In Self-realization, too, the Self is the center of the mandala. But this "Self-realized Self" is focused more on the center, though no less aware of, no less concerned with the surrounding personality. If the mandala were three-dimensional, then the Self-realized master would be penetrating deeper and deeper into the "Selfness" of the central point.

We will need to consider some Sanskrit terms in the following interpretation. Wherever possible, Sanskrit will be eschewed, but this will not always be possible. Often the English equivalent of a single Sanskrit word would require an entire paragraph.

The English word *man* is from the Sanskrit root *MAN*, which in turn is the root of the verb, "to think." Man, then, is named for his most characteristic attribute—intelligence. Furthermore, in the Eastern view the constitution of man is considered septenary—at one extreme *Sthula Sarira*, the gross physical body, at the other Atma, a ray of the universal spirit—the supreme soul. Different systems give different names to these principles and they are ordered in various ways. They are often divided into an upper triad and a lower quaternity. For our purposes it will suffice to classify the principles of man in the following manner which is similar to H.P. Blavatsky's scheme in *The Secret*

Doctrine, in which she introduces the Eastern view of man to the West.

Upper Triad:

ATMA

BUDDHI

HIGHER MANAS

Lower Quaternity:

LOWER MANAS OR KAMA-MANAS

PRANA

ETHERIC DOUBLE

PHYSICAL BODY

In this concept the upper triad consists of a ray of the divine soul (Atma), the human soul (Buddhi), and intuition and abstract or "higher" thought (Higher Manas). At the base of the lower quarternity are the physical body, the patterns that form it (Etheric Double), and the energies that sustain it (Prana). These are managed—or perhaps served would be more accurate, by Lower Manas, the everyday, working mind, the mind which serves carnal lust, which finds food, which drives cars—the mind without whose service we could neither live from day to day nor reach for upper triads of higher things: a Faithful Johannes indeed.

Not all men become aware of their higher triad. Of those who do, some "fall in love" with it, others kill it; still others, like the old king, are unable quite to do murder, but fearful of change—

120

for who knows what may happen—they lock it up
and try to forget that they ever saw it. Thus the
king in our story, sensing that he will be unable to
keep the forbidden room locked, calls Faithful
Johannes, his lower manas, and says: "Don't let
my son see the picture in that room, for if he does,
who knows what the future will be?"

Since all the characters in this story are aspects
of one man, what the king is saying is, "Don't let
me into that room; let me be conservative. I don't
want to grow—I'm happy the way I am." But of
course he's not happy, otherwise he wouldn't
have this dialogue with himself. He is old—he will
die—he must die, for he cannot stop that aspect of
himself which is the young prince from falling in
love with the Princess of the Golden Roof.

The young prince, the potential striving to
evolve, must have the help of his practical mind—
of Faithful Johannes—in whatever he does.

It is Faithful Johannes who tells the young
prince, now king, that all must be gold, that there
must be neither dross nor base metal; it is Faithful
Johannes who helps the king across the symbolic
sea; Faithful Johannes gently lures the princess;
and Faithful Johannes, after the princess has
agreed to marry and become one with the king,
"overhears the three ravens."

At this point we may profitably delve still deeper
into the symbology of the raven. H.P. Blavatsky

tells us a great deal, not merely that black birds are connected with primeval wisdom, but why this is so.

> What is the inner meaning of all these black birds? It is that they are all connected with the primeval Wisdom, which flows out of the pre-cosmic Source of All, symbolized by the Head, the Circle or the Egg; and they all have an identical meaning and relate to the primordial Archetypal Man, Adam Kadmon, the creative origin of all things. (2, vol 2, p. 161)

In search of information concerning a specific black bird, the raven, Blavatsky turns to the Kabbalah, from which we learn that its chief meaning is that of a new cycle, a new beginning. "Whatever the many other meanings of this emblematical allegory may be, its *chief* meaning is that of a new Cycle and a new Round" (2, vol 2, p. 161). Our three ravens are then wise messengers, symbols of a new round, of a new, more complete man.

As symbols of growth these birds are aware of the dangers: they know how easy it is to strangle growth, to kill new life. And practical lower manas, Faithful Johannes, knows too. Once the ship has docked and the symbolic sea journey is ended, back on earth there will be the chestnut horse of lust—of desire for all pleasures of the flesh. The bridal garment which seems so rich and desirable, but which will burn and destroy, also represents lust—lust for success and for material power. Certainly the Princess of the Golden Roof could not continue to live with either of these as a constant companion.

Even if the princess survives these dangers, she will die unless three drops of blood are sucked from her right breast. Both number and direction point to the masculine world of the everyday, a world in which the princess has tried too soon to take her place. Like an unvaccinated child exposed to smallpox, she will either die or be disfigured— unless the poison is sucked from her. Yet again Johannes is faithful—and for being faithful is turned to stone.

How often do we see people with no personal Faithful Johannes to guide and protect them—men and women who perhaps have married their per- sonal Princess (or Prince) of the Golden Roof and moved into another world? They are frequently quite delightful—in small doses; and just as fre- quently need help from someone else's Faithful Johannes.

The king is aware of something missing. He has his princess, they have their children, yet none of them are happy. King, queen, and royal children, all are facets of one individual—one incomplete individual, so incomplete that he is prepared to sacrifice those very children in order to bring Faithful Johannes back to life.

These royal children are the creative result of the union of the king and his Princess of the Golden

123

Roof and all that they symbolize. By smearing Faithful Johannes with their blood, the king is, in a sense, imbuing Faithful Johannes with that creative force. He is saying, "Yes, what we have done is wonderful, but on this level too, we need Faithful Johannes—I need Faithful Johannes."

It is Faithful Johannes who has shot the horse, burned the bridal shirt, decontaminated the queen. Faithful Johannes may be lower manas, but even as lower manas he can function without lust, be it carnal or material. He can, he *must*, be a partner in the nurturing of the new potential—the still greater self symbolized by the royal children. Their father, the king, must be accompanied by Faithful Johannes as he moves about his castle.

In years to come perhaps these children too will peep through a forbidden door—and Faithful Johannes will have new masters—who will be his old master, reaching once more for an upper triad. For if there is an end to this evolutionary journey, neither Faithful Johannes nor his king, nor indeed any who read their story, have as yet sighted it. Man touches his higher self—makes his higher self part of his day-to-day life—and as higher self becomes lower, new heights take shape—new doors are locked on new forbidden rooms, thereby guaranteeing that the young king will open the door and see the Princess of the Golden Roof.

12

The Hero Goes East
(Somerset Maugham, *The Razor's Edge*; Hermann Hesse, *Siddhartha*)

Yet when the Maharishee comes to my courtyard
with me a little later, my contentment suddenly
deserts me. This man has strangely conquered
me....He has taken me into the benign presence of
my spiritual self and helped me, dull westerner that I
am, to translate a meaningless term into a living and
beautiful experience.

Paul Brunton

Even before my mind was able to recognize the fact,
and still less to express it, the invisible halo of this
sage had been perceived by something in me deeper
than any words. Unknown harmonies awoke in my
heart....It was as if the very soul of India pene-
trated to the very depths of my own soul and held
mysterious communion with it. It was a call which
pierced through everything, rent it in pieces and
opened a mighty abyss.

Henri Le Saux

The above lines, written respectively by Paul Brunton and the Benedictine monk, Henri Le Saux, describe their individual encounters with an actual man, the Self-realized master, Sri Ramana Maharshi. The following lines are from Somerset Maugham's novel, *The Razor's Edge*:

> We were left alone and he looked at me
> without speaking. I don't know how long the
> silence lasted. It might have been for half an

125

> hour. I've told you what he looked like; what I
> haven't told you is the serenity that he irradi-
> ated, the goodness, the peace, the selflessness.
> I was hot and tired after my journey, but grad-
> ually I began to feel wonderfully rested. (21,
> p. 272)

Maugham describes the Indian holy man, Sri
Ganesha, who, like virtually all of his major characters, was based on a living person: Sri Ramana
Maharshi. The impact of his meeting with the
"Sage of Arunachala" was to stay with Maugham
for the rest of his days, and to inspire his most
successful novel.

The Razor's Edge is basically the story of the inner
and outer journeys of a young American, Larry
Darrell. As a result of his experiences in World
War I, he feels unable to marry his upper-middle
class fiancée, work at the "right" job, and enjoy the
comfortable existence of the "right" people. His
decades-long search for personal meaning takes
him from the U.S. to Europe, and from Europe to
India and the ashram of Sri Ganesha.

When we last see Larry, he is about to complete
his circle, or rather spiral: he intends returning to
America, becoming a New York taxi driver and living, in his own words, "With calmness, forbear-
ance, compassion, selflessness, and calmness."

Throughout *The Razor's Edge* Somerset Maugham
brilliantly juxtaposes Larry Darrell's inner journey
with the outer journey of another character, Elliott
Templeton. The former dedicates his life to search-

ing for "his" truth; the latter, having found "his" truth when still very young, dedicates his life to enjoying it. And Elliott's truth exists only to be enjoyed; for to him the only conceivable truth is outer truth; and the only things that can possibly matter, that can make life worth living, are outer things. His life is dedicated to saying the right things to the right people, while wearing the right clothes in the right place. At one time he discusses Heaven with the book's narrator. While Elliott professes to believe in Heaven, it is impossible for him to even consider that it might, just might, be constituted on democratic lines. How could it possibly be Heaven if the right people—people like him!— had to rub shoulders with the hoi polloi? That would be Hell.

It says much for the talent of Somerset Maugham that Elliott Templeton never appears as a ridiculous figure—in fact we rather like him. He is frequently generous and always considerate of the feelings of others. He enjoys helping people— the right people. He even tries to help Larry Darrell, although the latter is not, strictly speaking, one of the right people. In the final analysis Elliott Templeton is literally incapable of understanding Larry Darrell. But then Somerset Maugham did not create Elliott in order that he might understand. Elliott is at once metaphor and backdrop: because Elliott exists, we understand Larry better.

No such "reader's aid" exists in the case of *Siddhartha*. But none is needed, for in a sense the eponymous hero of Hermann Hesse's novel provides his own backdrop. We know his aspirations; and his journeys within and without provide a view of him, not only against those aspirations, but against an earlier or later face of himself.

Siddhartha is a Brahmin who, while still young and though excelling in the duties of the priestly caste, grows dissatisfied. It seems to him that in spite of all their knowledge and holy books and disciplines, there is one thing—one all-important thing—that the Brahmins do not know. Like Larry Darrell, Siddhartha will journey within and without in search of "his" truth.

He will become a Samana—a forest ascetic. He will seek the Buddha, but realize that, just as the Buddha has personally conquered his Self, so he, Siddhartha, must conquer his Self. He will make love to and love and be loved by the beautiful courtesan Kamala. He will become a rich, very successful merchant.

In the fullness of time he will awaken from his sensual life and return to the mighty river whose waters, many faces before, he symbolically crossed. As a ferryman, he will learn from the wise-simple man who once ferried him across to different lives; and, like his predecessor, he will learn from the river itself.

Both Larry Darrell and Siddhartha were born to privilege, however different that privilege may have been. Both surrendered their birthright. Both spiraled. Both found at least a measure of inner peace. Perhaps it is not insignificant that both elect to become ferrymen, one in a cab on New York streets, the other in an actual boat on an actual river. But in order to assess their impact in terms of our thesis, it is not enough merely to understand their fictional lives, we must know something of their authors, and, perhaps more importantly, of their readers.

Some writers rebel against their roots. Not so William Somerset Maugham. He was middle-class; his values were middle-class; his writing was—and is—middle-class. There is no unseemly emotion. If he walks through his novels, he keeps them at arm's length. He is always reasonable, always correct. In his *The Summing Up*, which is a collection of autobiographical notes and opinions rather than autobiography per se, he plainly states that there are aspects of a man's character which, along with certain actions and thoughts, should forever remain private. Most of Maugham's readers, certainly those of 1944, were either middle-class in fact, or middle-class in fancy. They would have applauded his gentlemanly reticence, his well-bred reserve.

In *The Razor's Edge* Somerset Maugham appears as himself. It is as a successful middle-class writer that he reacts to Larry Darrell, and he reacts not only for himself, but on behalf of all his readers; furthermore, he is perceived to react in the "right" way—i.e., the way his collective audience would react, or like to think it would react, in similar circumstances. As narrator, Maugham might be fas-

129

cinated by Larry, but he is much fonder of the far
less admirable Elliott Templeton. Elliott is more at
ease with Larry than are any of the other characters; he understands him better—though he still
can't quite understand him. His reaction to Larry
is akin to that of a successful, middle-aged, not
unsympathetic stockbroker: "Nice feller. Bit
strange mind you. Looking for something or other
I suppose. Still—damn glad he's not my son."

In time to come, *The Razor's Edge* will inspire two
film versions; it is destined to become its author's
most successful full-length novel. How clever was
Somerset Maugham? Was his "at-arm's-length"
approach to Larry Darrell deliberate? Did he
perhaps suspect that this might be the only
approach that the audience he was writing for
would find acceptable—would, in fact, understand?
Or did his writing merely reflect, quite accurately,
his own feelings and perception of the world?

In so far as they concern Somerset Maugham,
the answers to these questions can never be
known, and are unimportant anyway. But in terms
of our thesis—if we are to correctly position Larry
Darrell and Siddhartha on the spiral of heroes
which runs from Odysseus to Luke Skywalker—we
must come to terms, not merely with the dates on
which these characters first appeared, but with
their respective epochs.

The Razor's Edge was first published in 1944.
Although *Siddhartha* had been around for twenty-
two years, it would not be translated and published in English until 1951. In 1944 the British Raj

was alive and, if not well, at least not perceived as terminal. India, along with much of the rest of the world, was under English reign. If some were beginning to suspect that God might not actually be an Englishman, they knew that at the very least he was a Christian gentleman.

In retrospect it seems safe to say that in many ways 1944 had more in common with 1934, or even 1914, than with 1951. Somewhere in the seven years separating 1944 from 1951 a world died. A way of life, a system of certainties rather than mere beliefs—certainties which had held unchallenged sway for decade upon decade—was gone forever. 1951 was not seven years later. It was a different epoch.

How different was the old epoch from the new? Compare Larry Darrell talking about metempsychosis with a not dissimilar passage from *Siddhartha*. In *The Razor's Edge* Larry recounts a vision that comes to him while he is meditating in front of a candle flame in his little room at the ashram. He sees a long line of figures, the nearest being a kindly, mild lady in her seventies with lace cap and grey ringlets. Next is a gaunt, grim Jew, scholarly yet passionate. Next comes a sixteenth-century Englishman in court dress, with a bold and reckless look. Behind him stretch an endless queue of vague figures. They all fade away, and Larry speculates on their meaning:

> Of course it may be that I'd fallen into a doze and dreamt. It may be that my concentration on that feeble flame had induced a sort of hyp-

notic condition in me and that those three figures that I saw as distinctly as I see you were
recollections preserved in my subconscious. But
it may be that they were myself in past lives. It
may be that I was not so very long ago an old
lady in New England and before that a Levan-
tine Jew and somewhere back, soon after
Sebastian Cabot had sailed from Bristol, a gal-
lant at the court of Henry Prince of Wales.
(21, p. 266)

For Larry Darrell the quest per se is over. He has
found "his" truth. That he has done so is due in
no small measure to Sri Ganesha, the fictional
Ramana Maharshi. Yet even at this dramatic
moment, Maugham, whose writing is never emotional, remains uncommitted. He allows Larry to
reassure his readers: it may have been this reincarnation thing—but then again maybe Larry was just
tired, or hypnotized, or—

There is nothing unpleasant about Maugham's
cynicism, but it is always present—it underlines
every paragraph. Maugham is always the detached
observer, never the committed participant. That
which he chooses to reveal about himself in his
autobiographical fragments suggests that this was
true not merely of his writing, but of his life. In
which case we may conclude that, just as Nikos
Kazantzakis could not have created a Leopold
Bloom who held life at bay, and James Joyce could
not have created an Odysseus who was forever
reaching for more life, so Somerset Maugham
could not have created Hesse's Siddhartha. Siddhartha too had a vision—of hundreds and thousands of faces. Staring into the river, he saw the

face of a dying fish, a newly born child, a mur- ⌐ KEY
derer—as perpetrator and at the same time as victim of the executioner. He saw naked bodies in
postures of love, corpses, heads of animals,
Krishna and Agni.

> He saw all these forms and faces in a thou-
> sand relationships to each other, all helping
> each other, loving, hating and destroying each
> other and become newly born. Each one was
> mortal, a passionate, painful example of all
> that is transitory. Yet none of them died, they
> only changed, were always reborn, continually
> had a new face; only time stood between one
> face and another. And all these forms and
> faces rested, flowed, reproduced, swam past
> and merged into each other, and over them all
> there was continually something thin, unreal
> and yet existing, stretched across like thin glass
> or ice, like a transparent skin, shell, form or
> mask of water—and this mask was Siddhar-
> tha's smiling face. (14, p. 121)

For Siddhartha, like Larry, the quest itself is over.
The paths which the Brahmin's son and the American truth-seeker followed are not dissimilar. In
fact, the two men are very much alike.

Such is not the case with Maugham, the quali-
fied doctor, and Hesse, the high-school dropout.
As already noted, there is, in all of Maugham's
writing, a sense of the dilettante, of the detached,
uninvolved observer. This is never the case with
Hesse. He does not believe that there are thoughts
which should forever remain private. When he
writes about himself, he holds nothing back; he
invites you into his mind. He shares not merely

133

the facts of his life, but his dreams and fantasies; and as with Jung, this world within is often more real, more important, than the world without.

Nor does Hesse feel it necessary to cushion his audience, and indeed himself, in the same manner of Maugham, by providing a list of comforting alternatives. Hesse would be as incapable of detaching himself to provide alternatives as Maugham would be of attaching himself to provide total commitment. Artists like Hesse and Kazantzakis are forerunners. Professional writers like Somerset Maugham are not. The former can tell us what the world and we who live in the world will be like in years to come; the latter can show us the past or help us to see the present with clearer eyes. But they are never prophets. To see tomorrow they, with the rest of us, must wait for tomorrow's sun to rise.

Kazantzakis could start writing his Odyssey in 1924; Hesse could publish *Siddhartha* in 1922. But could Somerset Maugham have written *The Razor's Edge* in the 1920s? And, if he had, would the book have enjoyed the enormous success that it would be accorded a quarter of a century later? To be fair to Somerset Maugham, however, we should also ask about *Siddhartha* and "The Odyssey, A Modern Sequel." If they had made their English language appearance in the 1920s, would either have run to more than a single printing?

Perhaps after considering these questions, we will decide that the first question should not be,

"Could Somerset Maugham have?" but rather, "Given Somerset Maugham's keen perception of his contemporaries and understanding of their mores, would he, in the 1920s—however fascinated he might personally have been with Larry Darrell—have taken the time to write a full-length novel about him?"

If it is unlikely that either Hesse or Kazantzakis wondered, or even cared, what the world would think of their works, it is even more unlikely that Maugham did not. In fact, with his keen eye for the mores of his contemporaries, he would probably have known—in so far as it is possible to know these things—exactly what to expect. He could not, however, have conceived of the Beat Generation, nor could he have dreamed that a decade later such concepts as dharma and karma, Zen and Vedanta, individuation and Self-realization would not be merely understood in the West, but frequently embraced.

If our spiral of heroes was square rather than circular, it would be convenient to have Larry Darrell and Siddhartha meet at, say, the northeast corner. Being a square, there would be no messy overlapping of concepts. Somerset Maugham's detached alternatives would butt up against Hermann Hesse's attached convictions. We could step from one to the other without having to negotiate the uncomfortable curve of uncertainty.

But neither life, nor art, nor our spiral is that simple.

13

The Ripeness of Time

*As much an unthinking ritual as breathing—the
nightly patrol. Times beyond counting, he has been
as he is tonight: watching.*

The feature story in a recent publication opens
with the above quote. Were it not for this story
and others like it, we could have neatly wrapped
up our thesis. But the story and its genre must
somehow find a place on our spiral.

In the course of this story the following quotes
are among several used to underline the message:

> The tea ladle which passes through the heat
> and cold of hell has no mind and therefore
> suffers not.
>
> . . .
>
> To jump over the four big continents in one
> leap one must decipher the wind and unriddle
> the rain.
>
> . . .
>
> The oxen are slow, but the earth is patient.
>
> . . .
>
> The phoenix does not come; the river gives
> forth no chart.
>
> . . .
>
> If a man seeks to know thoroughly the past,
> the present, and the future, he should under-

stand that the realm of existence is but a creation of the mind.

. . .

Highest are those who are born wise. Next are
those who become wise by learning. After
them come those who have to toil painfully in
order to acquire learning. Finally, to the lowest
classes of the common people belong those
who toil painfully without ever managing to
learn.

At the end of this story the several sources of
these and other quotes are thus acknowledged as
quotations from: *The Analects of Confucius*, Chuang
Tzu, Zen Koans of various masters, Eric Hoffer,
Leslie Tommer, African sayings.

We shall return to the story in which these
quotes were featured. It appeared in a periodical
which has been a consistently high seller for the
best part of fifty years. Before we positively identify the periodical in question, the reader may care
to speculate, if not as to the exact title, then as to
the family, the genre, to which this story would
seem to belong.

Were it not for this story and others like it, we
could have imagined two vaguely parallel lines and
two spirals of dissimilar size, all having as their
origin the first Odysseus. One of our parallel lines
would contain the true-blue tradition of gentlemen
who always know what is and simply is not done.
These heroes neither lie nor cheat nor, so far as we
know, womanize. Their faces are unmarked by
warts, their minds untroubled by temptation to
commit even the most venial of sins. In our cynical

age, this line may be somewhat undernourished. But in comic books there will always be a super-hero; and in every television police station or general hospital, at least one character who is, and forever will be, true blue.

The line running parallel to True-Blue is a lot fatter, and on it Odysseus himself would feel right at home. On this line are 007 and a host of roguish adventurers. Chaucer has fed this line, and Bocaccio, and Balzac, and Peter Chenyney, and Harold Robbins, and—the list goes on. The popularity of this particular line tells us about our day and age, and it tells us about every day and age. Whether in fact or in fiction, mankind has always delighted in tales of liars, trenchermen, and adulterers. Shahrazad knew this, so did Shakespeare, so does Harold Robbins.

Though their evolution can be traced from Homer's Odysseus, no one could claim that such as Leopold Bloom could be located on the same straight line as he: the face of the hero has changed. Unlike Odysseus and James Bond, Bloom is not content to be merely Bloom and forever Bloom. He and others like him want desperately to be more, to do more—to individuate, to achieve Self-realization. But they have become part of the very matrix which ensnares them. If they spiral upward, they do so very slowly; more often they go round and round in the very same circle.

It has become fashionable and accepted as true that the Blooms of this world are victims of the twentieth century. But perhaps this explanation is a little too easy. It seems unlikely that all the poor men standing at the gates of all the rich men in "All Things Bright and Beautiful" spent much of their time in rejoicing in their lot. It is, however, just as unlikely that more than a very, very few of these unfortunates ever thought that perhaps they could actually change that lot. Whether or not they accepted that God had ordained their miserable existence, they accepted its inevitability: as the hymn so aptly tells us, dreams of becoming more were not encouraged.

Bloom's tragedy is that in an age which discounts inevitability, he managed no more than to become Bloom. Once, like James Joyce, he was Stephen Dedalus, and Stephen might, just might have become, if not Siddhartha, at least Larry Darrell. Instead he became that most dominant of twentieth-century creatures—a survivor.

We have finally entered an age in which survivors—some at any rate—have managed to do more than "live lives of quiet desperation." Furthermore, in this age the desire to be more—to grow spiritually, to "climb the mountain"—is not treated with quite as much amusement, even mocking scorn, as was once the case. That this is so is due in no small part to the changing face of the hero—which brings us back to the quotes with which this chapter opened.

The quotes in question appeared in the 567th issue of *Detective Comics*. This comic is dated October 1986, and the hero featured in the story in question is none other than our old friend Batman. Batman? The Caped Crusader? "The Analects of Confucius?" Wow! and Zap! and Kerboom! The face of the hero sure has changed! To get some idea of how much, let us imagine the kind of dialogue in which the name Confucius might have appeared in the same comic, say thirty-five years ago:

Robin: Holy Moley! Batman, those diamonds sure slipped through those crooks' fingers!

Batman: Well chum, you know that underworld slang for diamonds is ice!

Robin: Right, Batman! And Confucius he say, "ice velly slippery stuff!"

Batman: Ha, ha, ha!

If ever a hero could have been assumed to belong amid the square-jawed stalwarts of the line of True-Blue, surely that hero would have been Batman. Which is not to say that Batman is no longer square-jawed, stalwart and true-blue: Batman is still Batman. But what of the stories in which he appears? What of the concepts which surround him? If a publisher is to stay in business, he must find an audience and then cater to that audience. Comics today are doing very nicely thank you, which would indicate that not only is their audience ready to accept *The Analects of Con-*

fucius, but that they feel right at home among Zen Koans.

And lest we imagine that *Detective Comics* #567 is some kind of freak, consider the following quote from an article by Lloyd Rose, literary manager of a theater, which appeared in the August 1986 issue of *Atlantic Monthly:*

> [The comic] ''Ronin'' isn't fully successful, but it has its own peculiar power....The epony-mous hero is a samurai reincarnated into the body of an armless, legless, mental deficient who is used for testing new prosthetic devices.

Never mind the prosthetic devices or the armless, legless hero. What about the reincarnated Samurai? Not only is reincarnation appearing in a comic book, it is obviously being treated seriously (''Levitating Lamas, Batman!—Metempsychosis!''); and, it seems safe to speculate, being accepted at a serious, perhaps even a matter-of-fact level, by the comic's readers.

Rose's article is entitled ''Comic Books For Grown-Ups.'' But we have only to read a few pages to realize that, while some of the readers might by legal definition be ''grown-up,'' just as many by the same definition would be classed as minors.

In a recent conversation, a friend who is inter-ested in such things posed the following question: ''I wonder who has more affected our view of the

East, Bruce Lee or D.T. Suzuki?''[1] If for the latter
name he had substituted Paul Brunton, H.P.
Blavatsky, Paramhansa Yogananda, etc., the
implicit answer to his rhetorical question would
remain the same. Which brings us to hierarchies
and pyramids and time and the ripeness of time,
and perhaps—if we can bring all these together
with our lines and spirals—to an understanding of
the changing face of the hero.

It has been pointed out that change is hier-
archic—that there has to be one Buddha before
there can be a hundred million Buddhists. While
this is self-evident, we should bear in mind that
pyramids are built from the ground up, and that
there is a world of difference between a charismat-
ic guru and a truly messianic figure. The latter may
well attract apostles, who will attract disciples,
who will attract half the world. The former, however right and timely and just their message may
be, seldom attract more than a relatively small
following—however enlightened that following may
be. If East and West are finally to come together,
perhaps it is essential that we build a pyramid,
and that our building blocks are heroes whose
faces are changing and changing and ever-chang-
ing...

Finally, if we consider our heroes against time,
we will see that such a concept is not without

---

[1] Bruce Lee was a famous movie actor and master of Kung Fu.
D.T. Suzuki was a Japanese scholar who taught at Columbia
University and was influential in spreading Zen Buddhism in
the West.

precedent. The people, the base of the pyramid, have always been of the hero's time. As above, so below; as in life so in literature; as in the journey within and without of the disciple, so in the journey within and without of Everyman. When the disciple is ready the teacher appears. When Everyman is ready, the face of the hero changes.

Bibliography

1. Black Elk. 1984. *Black Elk's Account of the Seven Rites of the Oglala Sioux.* Recorded and edited by Joseph Epes Brown. New York: Penguin.
2. Blavatsky, H.P. 1971. *The Secret Doctrine.* 6 Volumes. Adyar Edition. Madras, India: Theosophical Publishing House.
3. Blavatsky, H.P. 1973. *Theosophical Glossary.* Los Angeles: The Theosophy Co.
4. Brunton, Paul. 1972. *A Search in Secret India.* New York: Samuel Weiser, Inc.
5. Cambell, Joseph. 1969. *The Hero With A Thousand Faces.* Mountain View, California: World Publishing Co.
6. Cirlot, J.E. 1971. *A Dictionary of Symbols.* New York: Philosophical Library.
7. Coward, Harold. 1985. *Jung and Eastern Thought.* Albany, New York: SUNY Press.
8. Dante. 1947. *The Divine Comedy.* Laurence Binyon, tr. New York: Viking Press.
9. Edwards, Thomas. "The Odyssey, A Modern Sequel," in *The Whole Earth Times*, January, 1971, p. 29.
10. Ginsberg, Allen. 1959. *Howl and Other Poems.* San Francisco: City Lights Books.
11. Graves, Robert. 1968. *The Greek Myths.* 2 Volumes. New York: Pelican Books.
12. Gray, Eden. 1971. *Mastering the Tarot.* New York: Crown Publishers.
13. Grimm, Jakob and Wilhelm. 1977. *Grimm's Tales for Young and Old.* Ralph Manheim, tr. New York: Doubleday and Co.

Bibliography

14. Hesse, Hermann. 1951. *Siddhartha.* New York: New Directions.
15. Hitchcock, General Ethan Allen. 1977. *The Red Book of Appin.* Los Angeles: Philosophical Research Society.
16. Homer. 1961. *The Odyssey.* Robert Fitzgerald, tr. New York: Doubleday and Co.
17. Jung, C.G. *Collected Works.* Volumes 5, 9 (parts 1 and 2), 12, 13, 14, 15. Bollingen Series. Princeton, New Jersey: Princeton University Press.
18. Jung, C.G., ed. 1964. *Man and His Symbols.* New York: Doubleday and Co.
19. Kazantzakis, Nikos. 1958. *The Odyssey: A Modern Sequel.* Kimon Friar, tr. New York: Simon and Schuster.
20. Levitt, Morton P. 1980. *The Cretan Glance: The World and Art of Nikos Kazantzakis.* Columbus: Ohio State University Press.
21. Maugham, W. Somerset. 1984. *The Razor's Edge.* New York: Penguin Books.
22. Mead, G.R.S. 1966. *Fragments of a Faith Forgotten.* Secaucus, New Jersey: University Books.
23. Merton, Thomas. "News of the Joyce Industry." *The Sewanee Review 77.* Summer, 1969.
24. Miller, Henry. 1959. *The Henry Miller Reader.* Laurence Durrell, ed. New York: New Directions.
25. Nichols, Sallie. 1982. *Jung and Tarot: An Archetypal Journey.* New York: Samuel Weiser.
26. Nietzsche, Friedrich. 1974. *The Birth of Tragedy.* New York: Gordon Press.
27. Nietzsche, Friedrich. 1972. *Thus Spoke Zarathustra.* Walter Kaufmann, tr. New York: The Viking Press.
28. Ovid. 1958. *The Metamorphoses.* Horace Gregory, tr. New York: Mentor Books.
29. Pound, Ezra. 1960. *Literary Essays of Ezra Pound.* Winchester, Massachusetts: Faber and Faber, Ltd.
30. Prevelakis, Pandelis. 1961. *Nikos Kazantzakis and His Odyssey. A Study of the Poet and the Poem.* New York: Simon and Schuster.

Bibliography

31. Shakespeare, William. *Hamlet.*
32. Staley, Thomas, and Benstock, Bernard, Editors. 1970. *Approaches to Ulysses: Ten Essays.* Pittsburgh: University of Pittsburgh Press.
33. Tolstoy, Leo. 1974. *War and Peace.* Rosemary Edwards, tr. 2 Volumes. New York: Penguin Books.
34. Van der Post, Sir Laurens. 1975. *Jung and the Story of Our Time.* New York: Pantheon Books.
35. Von Franz, Marie-Louise. 1974. *Shadow and Evil in Fairy Tales.* Dallas: Spring Publications.

About the Author

Rodney Standen, Ph.D., is a former script writer and also wrote advertising copy. He served as head scenario writer for a division of Twentieth Century Fox, where he also wrote weekly newsreels. He worked in various capacities, including production manager, in the British film industry, and has been associated with independent film producers. He was twice awarded a diploma at the Cannes Film Festival for commercials that he wrote.

Born in Johannesburg, South Africa, he was educated there. More recently, he earned the Ph.D. degree from Somerset University in England, which is an Associated Educational Institution of UNESCO, and this book is based on his thesis. He is presently teaching English to Sioux and Assiniboine Indians at a tribal college in Poplar, Montana, where he resides with his wife Ilene.

More quality Quest Books—

ABRIDGEMENT OF THE SECRET DOCTRINE—
Ed. by Elizabeth Preston & Christmas Humphreys
A 260 page abridgement of the original three-volume
magnum opus *by H. P. Blavatsky.*

GIFTS OF THE LOTUS—Ed. by Virginia Hanson
A "pocket or purse" Quest miniature.
366 meditations drawn from spiritually oriented
philosophers such as Plato, Emerson, Annie
Besant, Sri Aurobindo.

MASTERING THE PROBLEMS OF LIVING—
By Haridas Chaudhuri
Overcome depression. Conquer anxiety.
Make decisions.

REINCARNATION: FACT OR FALLACY?—
By Geoffrey Hodson
A clairvoyant studies the question of rebirth.

SPECTRUM OF CONSCIOUSNESS—
By Ken Wilber
An overview of psycho-therapies, the non-duality
of spirit, the unique value of all religions.

THOUGHT FORMS—
By A. Besant and C. W. Leadbeater
A book full of colors to enable you to match
your aura to your mood.

Available from:

The Theosophical Publishing House
306 West Geneva Road
Wheaton, IL 60187